THE GR

ORGANIC
WINE
GUIDE

THE GREAT
ORGANIC
WINE
GUIDE

HILARY WRIGHT

PIATKUS

For Ian

First published in 2000 by
Judy Piatkus (Publishers) Ltd
5 Windmill Street
London W1P 1HF

A catalogue record for this book is available from the British Library

ISBN 0 7499 1998 1

Edited by Anne Lawrance
Designed by Sara Kidd
Typeset by Action Publishing Technology Limited, Gloucester
Printed and bound in Great Britain by
Mackays of Chatham PLC

ACKNOWLEDGEMENTS

Severe thanks are due to the following: Ian Wright, for tenacious research and, as usual, for having the original idea (he has witnesses this time). Colin Alston, for reading the manuscript with an unerring eye for where I wasn't on the nail and pointing it out with grace. Liz Trubridge, Carolyn Boyes and Dani Glover, for positive and helpful feedback on various sections of the text. Colleagues Tim Atkin, Jancis Robinson, Joanna Blythman, Lisa Barnard, Andrew Jefford, Phillippe Boucheron, Deh-Ta Hsiung and Sally Easton MW for much help with transgenics. Winemakers Richard Doughty, James Millton and Rainer Lingenfelder, who tirelessly answered my questions. Michael Palij MW, for sight of his dissertation. Michael Wynne, for the ice cream and motivational stories of launderettes. Barnaby 'Toon Army' Wenner, for being. Elaine, Alex and Rachel James, for sanctuary. And Chris Howe, without whom ...

A special thanks to everyone who helped by giving me information about producers and letting me taste their wines, particularly Lance Pigott and Neil Palmer at Vintage Roots, Jem Gardener and David Gill MW at Vinceremos, HDRA and Tony Mason at the Organic Wine Company, Trevor Hughes at T&W Wines, and Richard Gauntley, of Gauntleys of Nottingham, who proved that there is organic life in Alsace. To Liz Robertson MW, and Jackie Gear of the HDRA; also Caroline Carrick, Joanne Lemon, Ruth Chadwick, Sara Hately, Sarah Groves, Alex Gilson, and all the other PR and marketing persons who so tirelessly and helpfully answered all my questions. And to Rachel Winning, my editor, whose cheerful willingness to communicate by all available means with a globetrotting author went far beyond the call of duty.

Gladys Horiuchi of the Californian Wine Institute offered much helpful information, as did Julia Schregel of the German Wine Information Service. Geoffrey Kelly of Austria, Colin Deane of Bacchus (Greek to you and me), Kate Sweet Brown-Forman and Jane Hughes of Southcorp were all splendidly helpful. Andrew Lorand and Cheryl Kemp, too. And Mahalo nui loa to everyone at Kahumana. Amama.

Finally, very special thanks to Catherine, Dani, Debbie, Deena, Donna, Eileen, Fiona, Gayle, Gretel, Jay, Jane, June, Kay, Kirti, Margaret, Neil, Nicky, Rory, Simonne, Terry and Victoria, without whom this book would have been finished much sooner.

CONTENTS

Introduction: the truth about wine   1

1   Why choose organic wine?   9
2   Definitions of organic: black and white or shades of grey?   16
3   Organic wine versus conventional wine in the vineyard   28
4   Winery wizardry: techniques that separate organic and
    conventional winemakers   50
5   Genetic manipulation and modification: how it affects
    vines   63
6   Biodynamics: healing the vineyard   73
7   Where's it coming from? A country-by-country guide   88
8   Who to buy from and how to buy with confidence   107
9   Bringing it all back home: all the wine that's fit to drink
    (and some that isn't)   126

A final word   186
Glossary   187
Useful addresses and websites   197
Index   200

INTRODUCTION:
THE TRUTH ABOUT WINE

THE FIRST TIME I stood in an organic vineyard I knew it was different. There were flowers growing between the rows of vines, flowers in full bloom. The air was alive with the sound of buzzing insects, insects that lived among the flowers, zooming around the vines searching out the pests that prey on grapes. I was witnessing nature's system of checks and balances in full operation. The vines themselves turned their leaves to the sun, with a sheen on the leaves I hadn't seen in conventional vineyards. Above all, there was a different atmosphere – of life, of vitality. It was such an exciting moment.

From then on, I wanted to know more. I began to discover that many of the wines I most enjoyed drinking – wines with flavour, character, personality – were made by winemakers who grew their grapes organically. What were they doing that made the difference? I began to ask questions. Around this time I was writing books about travelling to France to buy wine direct from winemakers. I wanted to write about people you'd enjoy visiting – men and women making the best wines of their region, allowing the grapes to express their personality and a sense of place, reflecting the weather conditions of the year in which they grew. And, surprise surprise, most of the producers I chose were growing their grapes organically – even if they didn't say so on the label. When I asked what motivated them to work in this way, the answers they gave were varied. Some felt simply that organic methods made wines of a purer, clearer flavour. Some told horror stories about their experiences with chemicals. Many talked about wanting to farm the

1

land in a sustainable, earth-friendly way, so they could hand on their land to their children in the best possible condition.

But the sad truth is that working in harmony with the land, avoiding chemicals, is still the exception rather than the rule. Conventional winemakers – and that means the vast majority of those making wine – spray the grapes with a terrifying array of chemicals that kill bees and butterflies as well as predators. They spray fungicides to stop mildew and rot. They spray herbicides to kill off the weeds that grow between vine rows, which might compete with the vines for nutrients.

All these chemicals fall into the soil and poison the ground water. They are toxic to the people who spray them so they have to wear protective clothing to work the land. And what of the chemical residues that might remain in the wine we drink? Is this the way we really want to live?

Choosing organic wine is not only better for our health, it delivers a clear message to those who make the wine that we will no longer tolerate this indiscriminate use of chemicals.

This book tells you the truth about how conventional wine is made. It also tells you what alternatives there are, in other words what the organic grape growers do to produce great grapes that make the sort of wine you and I want to drink – wine with bags of flavour and no lurking additives. Now I'm not suggesting that all wines made organically will automatically have more flavour and character than all wines made conventionally. I'm not promising that you'll always find a great organic wine wherever you look. But I do know that the further up the quality ladder you go, the more likely it is that the wine will be made organically. Nearly all the top producers follow organic methods, whether or not they admit to it, because they have learned from experience that showering the vineyard with chemicals is the best way to dumb down a wine. They want the character of their wine to speak for itself, and they know organic principles give them the best means of doing that.

WHAT THIS BOOK WILL TELL YOU

It isn't always easy to find organic wine. For one thing, it's rare to find large estates farming organically. Most organic producers are still small, family-run operations, and they don't make enough wine for the supermarkets to put the bottles on every shelf. That's why you'll find a wider selection from the specialist wine merchants listed in this book – small is most definitely beautiful in this case.

Another key reason is that many producers who are certified organic don't declare that fact on the label. They have many reasons for this, some valid, some less so, and I'll go into that in more detail later on. So it used to be really difficult to find out just who was making wine organically. That's where this book will help out, by telling you what you need to know to make an informed choice.

It covers:

- why choose organic wine?
- taste – is it really any different?
- why producers go organic
- definitions of 'organic' – black and white or shades of grey?
- organic wine versus conventional wine in the vineyard
- winery wizardry – techniques that separate organic and conventional winemakers
- genetic manipulation and modification – how it affects vines
- biodynamic grape growing – healing the vineyard
- where organic wine is made, worldwide
- who sells organic wine?
- tasting notes on over 150 organic wines
- useful addresses and websites
- glossary

WHY CHOOSE ORGANIC WINE?

You might be looking for clean, pure flavour. You might want to avoid poisonous pesticide residues or genetically modified organisms. You might be looking for wines with lower sulphur levels – sulphur is a notorious inducer of hangovers. You might want to support producers who grow sustainably, ecologically and have respect for the land. You might be bored with the fact that wines are all starting to taste the same, and be looking for a wine with character and personality.

TASTE – IS IT REALLY ANY DIFFERENT?

This is one you can argue about, largely because wine is created in two stages – growing the grapes and then making the wine. And it's perfectly possible to grow spanking top-quality grapes then mess it all up in the winery and produce duff stuff. But some very respected wine writers have already said that well-made organic wine can have a better taste, and we'll look at the arguments that say that organic flavour is better than conventional.

WHY PRODUCERS GO ORGANIC

Some grape growers have been farming organically for generations. It's the way their parents and grandparents worked, and they saw no reason to go down the chemical sprays route.

Others have noticed that their vines have been weakened by years of dependence on sprays, and that the intensive use of chemicals has turned their soil from a vibrant living collection of micro-organisms into inert, dead matter, unable to support life.

Many have realised the damage that intensive use of fertilisers is doing to the water we drink, and how pesticides affect wildlife and birds, and they want to farm more in harmony with nature.

And yes, others have realised that consumers are increasingly demanding organic food and wine. There's an expanding market here and some producers are jumping on the bandwagon for economic rather than philosophical reasons. But many of these economic converts then find that organic methods help them produce better wine that sells at a higher premium, which convinces them still further.

DEFINITIONS OF 'ORGANIC' – BLACK AND WHITE OR SHADES OF GREY?

The term 'organic' is defined in law. Anyone putting the word 'organic' on their wine label has to sign up to one of the many certifying bodies and submit to regular scrutiny.

I found, however, that in addition to those winemakers who are certified organic there are many who do farm organically but don't say so on the label, or sign up to one of the certifying bodies. This chapter looks at the reasons why.

ORGANIC WINE VERSUS CONVENTIONAL WINE IN THE VINEYARD

Grape growing – viticulture – the conventional way relies heavily on intensive use of chemical pesticides and artificial fertilisers. Organic viticulture, on the other hand, refuses to use chemical interventions. Growing grapes organically means focusing your attention on creating healthy, living soil which can support healthy, naturally resistant vines.

This is where organic wine is created – in the vineyard. The difference between conventional and organic grape growers' methods – what they do or don't do, and why – lies at the heart of the organic debate. I'll explain exactly what the different approaches are at every stage.

WINERY WIZARDRY – TECHNIQUES THAT SEPARATE ORGANIC AND CONVENTIONAL WINEMAKERS

Some aspects of organic winemaking – vinification – have different and more stringent regulations than conventional winemaking. For example, the difference between organic and non-organic practices on the addition of sulphur is very clear-cut.

In other areas, such as whether or not the wine is filtered to remove all the tiny particles suspended in it, the decisions have less to do with being organic and more to do with making top-quality wine. We'll cover these issues in detail, too, because they are crucial to the quality of what's in the glass, and will help you make informed choices about the wine you want to drink.

GENETIC MANIPULATION AND MODIFICATION – HOW IT AFFECTS VINES

Genetic manipulation is all about cloning. While sheep have only recently emerged from the test tube, vines have been producing cloned identical siblings for decades. Many modern vineyards are planted from very few clones, and I'll discuss the dangers of this.

Genetic modification is a new danger. Inserting genes from unrelated species into the food we eat is heralded by the drugs companies producing them as a huge step forward. But is it really? This chapter looks at the terrifying changes being made to plants in the name of profit, starting with faster-growing annual crops and then looking at the slower-growing vines.

BIODYNAMIC GRAPE GROWING – HEALING THE VINEYARD

Biodynamic grape growing is, to my mind, the most exciting aspect of organics. It is catching on fast with some of the most forward-thinking young winemakers.

Biodynamics reaches a step beyond organics. It recognises that the earth is decreasing in fertility thanks to overuse of chemicals and a reluctance by conventional growers to nurture the soil as the bedrock of all plant growth and life. It seeks to harness all the energy forces available to us – not just the sun, but the moon and the planets – and to work in harmony with all these energy sources to restore the earth. It also uses herbal sprays, similar to homeopathy, to boost the natural health and strength of the vines.

Biodynamics requires a lot more dedication and commitment than organic grape growing – which itself is arduous – not least because, to work in harmony with all the planetary forces, you can only do certain work at certain times. This awareness of all cosmic energies sometimes causes those with a strictly materialistic approach to poke fun at those who work biodynamically, but it's heartening to see how many of these sceptics are gradually becoming converted as they discover for themselves that these methods work.

WHERE ORGANIC WINE IS MADE, WORLDWIDE

Some countries have a climate more conducive to growing organically than others. In a nutshell: hot dry good; cool damp bad. Some have governments throwing money at organic conversion. Some pooh-pooh the whole idea, claiming they don't need it. This chapter looks at who's making what, where, and why, and if you can expect more organic wine to emerge from these regions in the future.

WHO SELLS ORGANIC WINE?

I was amazed to find how much organic wine was available when I really started delving into the UK market. Supermarkets were caught on the hop in the spring of 1999, when the truth about genetic modification began to come out. Now, of course, most of them have at least one or two organic wines on their shelves, and that's to be applauded. But wouldn't you prefer a selection of one or two *hundred* organic wines? There are two first-class organic mail-order specialists who offer a really comprehensive range. Their addresses are included here, and I select the best of their wines and others in Chapter 9. You'll also find information on many other stockists who include organic or biodynamic wines in their lists.

TASTING NOTES ON OVER 150 ORGANIC WINES

You want to know which organic wines are worth buying? This section tells you. Divided by price, colour and country, I've given my honest assessment of a wide range of organic wines – including a few turkeys.

USEFUL ADDRESSES AND WEBSITES

Many organic winemakers now have websites where you can find out more about the wines they make. You can often e-mail any questions or comments direct to the winemaker. Several campaigning organisations also have useful websites.

GLOSSARY

In case there's an expression for which the meaning isn't entirely clear, I've included lists of both general and tasting terms.

1
WHY CHOOSE ORGANIC WINE?

PEOPLE SEEK OUT organic wine for different reasons. For many consumers, taste is paramount: organic wines can have a clean, pure flavour, reflecting the place and year that produced them. They're more likely to be wines showing real character and personality. And to buy organic is to support grape growers who work sustainably, respecting the earth and the environment.

Buying organic wines means you'll be avoiding any genetically modified organisms. Organic wines also contain less sulphur than most conventionally made wines – so, glass for glass, you're less likely to have a headache the morning after. This means they are also better for asthmatics at risk of allergic reactions to sulphur.

Most importantly perhaps, buying organic wine is the only way you can be sure of avoiding all the unspeakable chemicals that many conventional grape growers shower on their crop. It is quite extraordinary how much freedom conventional growers have to spray their crops with dozens of noxious chemicals, many of which are proven carcinogens (cancer-causing agents). What does it say about the state of modern viticulture when vineyard workers have to dress up like astronauts in protective clothing to apply these chemicals? We are consuming the residues of these. And at the same time we're poisoning the earth.

THE DANGERS OF CHEMICALS

Many consumers want to go back to values of respect for the earth and for animals. They have an abhorrence of intensive farming, of cruelty and insensitivity to livestock, and of poisoning the earth, themselves, and their children.

For others, it's a matter of safety. Chemicals are released into the food chain with insufficient testing, piling up after-effects in the soil and in our bodies decades before somebody finally realises the danger and bans them. I remember my grandfather, body completely unprotected, spraying his orchard with the insecticide DDT, a compound that now fills us with horror. DDT residues remain in the bodies of each one of us, despite the fact it was banned for its toxicity decades ago. Even polar bears, thousands of miles from agricultural centres, have absorbed traces of it. It's ineradicable.

The lessons of DDT clearly haven't been learned. Or of BSE, for that matter – a disease we were assured couldn't leap across species from mad cows to humans. Now, not content with infecting cows by feeding them unnatural foodstuffs, we're re-engineering our own food. No one knows what genetically modified crops will do to us in the long term, yet they have already been released into the world. Scientists using genetically modified organisms are tinkering with the building blocks of life with abandon. Moving away from this adulteration to something more actively healthy seems to be a positive step – not just in the food we eat, but in the wine we drink too. Drinking organic wine is about choice; choice to support winemakers who produce their wines with respect for themselves, their land and the future.

Choosing organic wine, and insisting on being offered it in our local supermarkets, is one means at our disposal to put a stop to this chemical-based madness. We can all take heart from the lessons of genetic modification learned in the spring of 1999. As the truth about these foods gradually became known, one supermarket after another caved in to public pressure – that's you and me – and withdrew the products from their shelves. Even Tesco, which stood out in solitary defiance of the public mood, eventually had to follow the others' lead.

Look how much more organic food there is on the shelves

compared to 12 months ago. The supermarkets were all caught on the hop and had at most two or three organic wines on their shelves. I'll wager that by the time you read this there will be many more available, with the promise of more to come.

There are good reasons, though, for looking further afield than the local supermarket to source your organic wine, and I'll be explaining why in a later chapter. I'll also be looking in some detail at just what it is that conventional growers do to their grapes and their wine, and how organic growers do it differently. Armed with this information, you can make a really informed choice about what you want to drink.

TASTE – IS IT REALLY ANY DIFFERENT?

Some people think so. The respected wine writer Robert Joseph, in a *Sunday Telegraph* article in December 1998, summed it up acutely: 'Observing organic principles does not, of course, guarantee that a wine will taste any better; but the care and attention that are called for when the chemicals are taken out of farming do seem to make good winemakers even better.'

Jilly Goolden also waxed lyrical on the TV programme *Food and Drink*. After reviewing a selection of organic wines priced between £3.99 and £13.99 she concluded: 'If this is what organic wines are like, I'm going to be looking for these labels in the supermarket much more.'

It's not that *any* wine produced organically is bound to be better than one which isn't. I wish that were true, but alas it ain't necessarily so. It's perfectly possible to screw up your winemaking even if you've grown your grapes organically. In fact, I'd go so far as to say that organic producers have to be more skilled than conventional ones. They have to be closely attuned to potential problems and take steps to avoid them almost before they've begun – certainly before they've taken hold. It's easy for a conventional producer to sit back and simply spray when insect infestation threatens to overwhelm the vines, for instance, or add chemicals to make a wine less acidic to compensate for under-ripe and acidic grapes, harvested too soon, because panic over a gloomy weather forecast set in. Preventative measures are harder work and require greater commitment. Organic producers have to pay more attention.

Avoiding chemical sprays means the land and the vines are not poisoned. So you can argue that the flavour will be a purer, more vivid expression of the grape. Building soil fertility and the vine's natural resistance to disease strengthens the grapes and allows them to speak more clearly of the soil, the variety, the climate. Allowing the wine to ferment and mature as it wishes to, rather than imposing a winemaker's will on it and forcing it to develop in a certain way, is also likely to make for better, richer, more complex wine. It simply needs patience to create it.

This patience, and the hands-off approach, means the wine can reflect the vintage – the amount of sun and rain the grapes had that year – and the climate, and the tender loving care the winemaker has given the vines. These are some of the key factors that allow wine to develop a character and style that make it unique.

As you might expect, people who specialise in selling organic wine believe in its taste advantages. Lance Pigott, of Vintage Roots, one of the top two organic wine sellers, feels that organic wines do taste fresher and show the grape variety to good advantage: 'They're very honest with your tastebuds. There's more difference between the years with organic wines, which is what a wine should be like. A lot of modern wines are made to a similar style every year, it doesn't matter what the harvest is like, good harvest or bad harvest, they're very much on an even keel. I think that's part of the mass production of wine.'

WINE IS GOOD FOR YOU – OFFICIAL (AND HOW TO PERSUADE YOURSELF THAT ORGANIC WINE IS EVEN BETTER)

After years of being told that even one glass of wine a day puts us on the slippery slope to squelching alcoholism, isn't it heartening to be told that wine is good for us? There have now been many studies into what has been dubbed the 'French Paradox'. It seems that the French can eat a diet high in saturated fat but have fewer heart attacks than the rest of the West.

World Health Organisation data shows that dairy fat is highly correlated with coronary heart disease (CHD) mortality. The more dairy fat you eat, the more likely you are to suffer from heart disease. Inhabitants of certain French cities, on the other hand, displayed very high fat consumption but low CHD mortality rates. The French men in the study smoked more, exercised less, and ate 30 per cent more fat – butter, lard, cheese, foie gras – yet had between a third and a half as many heart attacks as their American counterparts. This is the French Paradox. No wonder the Americans got upset, and began to research the reasons.

BETTER RED THAN DEAD

Wine was shown to be one of the few dietary factors to correlate with reduced CHD mortality, fruit consumption being another. The lowest mortality rates occur with moderate alcohol consumption, defined as one to three drinks a day, though mortality for heavy drinkers is higher than for non-drinkers. Everything in moderation, obviously. Wine appears to offer better protection than other forms of alcohol, and red wine seems to offer more benefits than white.

The ingredients that make the difference are found in grape skins, and red wines have more contact with the skins during the winemaking process. White grapes are crushed, then the juice is racked (siphoned) off the skins straight away and fermented. Red grapes, if they're going to be used to make red wine, will be crushed and then fermented as a job lot, skins and all, so that the skins gradually impart colour and tannins to the clear flesh and juice. This is why you can make white wine from red grapes but you can't make red wine from white grapes. Champagne, for instance, is largely made from red grapes (Pinot Noir and Pinot Meunier) but the juice is racked off the skins immediately after crushing, so next to no colour is imparted. So for maximum benefit, the future is red.

The Australians cottoned on to the health properties of wine long before this. Convicts carted across the world to begin a new life courtesy of HM Government were sometimes saved from scurvy by drinking wine. (Now there's something they didn't tell me at school …)

The doctors accompanying the convict ships, convinced during the voyage of the medicinal benefits of wine, planted vineyards in their new homeland which provided them with wine and also formed early exports back to Britain. And their names were Penfold, Lindeman … names we still see on wine labels today.

Modern Australia even has the sense not to make pregnant women feel bad about taking a glass. In 1989, a study advised: 'To stop moderate alcohol consumption caused unnecessary guilt and anguish and was counter-productive: up to two standard drinks a day was not associated with any foetal ill-effects.' They've even managed to persuade the Aussie government that a tax on wine is a tax on health. Imagine telling that to the Chancellor of the Exchequer. It gets a bit technical after that, really, though there's some interesting stuff about antioxidants in wine slowing artery clogging. All I need to know is that wine is good for me. And of course if it's organic I'm avoiding pesticides too. Pass the glass.

AVOIDING HIGH LEVELS OF SULPHUR
(AND A HANGOVER)

Sulphur is routinely added to wine to preserve it. It's one of the few chemical additives permitted in organic winemaking, because it is just about the only way of making sure the wine will stay good in the bottle. Many conventional winemakers also spray sulphur on their vines as well, to prevent fungal disease. So by the time the wine is finally bottled there's a good chance it has received a pretty high dose of the stuff.

This is bad news for asthma sufferers, who can develop an allergic reaction to sulphur. In the US in the 1980s salad bars were using very high concentrations of sulphur dioxide to stop the fruit salad and lettuce on display turning brown. This caused some serious asthmatic reactions, so in 1986 the Federal Drug Administration banned the use of sulphurs on fresh fruit and vegetables, and ordered all other food products to state their sulphite levels on the packaging.

This is where organic wine scores over the conventionally made product: organic wines have lower permitted maximum sulphur levels than conventional wines. Many people seek out organic wines for precisely that reason. I should mention that there are suggestions that some organic wines breach these regulations and contain excessive sulphur, which is why I support the move for wine back labels to declare their added ingredients, including sulphur levels. At present, idiotically, it's actually illegal to give this information on a wine bottle.

Regardless of the analysis, though, there is more than enough anecdotal evidence to suggest it's sulphur that gives you a morning-after headache. Many people firmly believe that organic wines are less likely to give you a hangover, and have lengthy tales of their own experiences to prove it. And while I can't think of any way of measuring this scientifically – my brain-numbing migraine may be your slight headache – I'm convinced that the better quality of wine I drink, the less likely I am to feel damaged by it the following morning. Like they say, life is just too short to drink bad wine.

2
DEFINITIONS OF ORGANIC:
BLACK AND WHITE OR SHADES OF GREY?

I KNOW THE word 'organic' is a misnomer, I know we are all organic compounds and nobody could eat inorganic food, but, hey, I didn't choose it. 'Organic' *is* rather an odd word to use to describe a naturally made product, because 'organic' simply means 'carbon-based' which all earth life-forms are.

The European Union (EU) has laid down precise regulations defining what can legally be called 'organic'. At present this covers grapes but not wine. There is no list of permitted ingredients and processing aids for wine. This means you can, in theory, make wine any way you like and still put 'organic' on the label (though there are regulations governing the maximum amount of sulphur you can add).

Curious. My man at the Ministry of Agriculture was of the opinion that the lack of rules stems from 'some reluctance amongst conventional growers to agree organic standards which might in some way cast doubt on existing conventional oenological [wine-making] practices'. He also pointed to the complexity of wine labelling rules which make it difficult for all the various interested parties to agree. He's optimistic, however, that 'continued pressure from the marketplace, where "organic wines" are becoming increasingly popular, will eventually result in standards being set'.

Meanwhile he uses inverted commas with the term 'organic wine' because, legally speaking, until there are standards for ingredients and processes there is no such product. It's more correct, legally, to say 'wine made from organically grown grapes'. And naturally we want to keep it legal.

So let's agree terms here. By 'organically grown grapes' I mean grapes grown without the application of synthetic fertilisers, pesticides and other chemical sprays. And in the winery I expect minimum mucking-about, low sulphur levels, and if possible no fining or filtering. So here's the definition I've used throughout my research:

wine produced from organically grown grapes, with minimum chemical intervention in the winery.

I'll be taking that as the standard definition throughout this book.

Unfortunately, rather than taking a Europe-wide view and setting out a single set of regulations that covered the whole of the European winemaking fraternity, the EU opted to authorise the already existing certifying bodies in each member state, such as the Soil Association in the UK. This can lead to minor anomalies in what does or doesn't legally constitute an organic wine, because some certifiers are rumoured to be more lenient than others; but it was certainly cheaper than setting up a new standards agency, which was probably the rationale behind the decision.

WHAT ABOUT WINES THAT MIGHT BE ORGANIC BUT AREN'T CERTIFIED?

All wines wanting to use the word 'organic' on the label must be certified organic through one of the national certifying bodies. So get certified and declare yourself organic on the label. What could be simpler? Except, of course, that winemakers are an idiosyncratic bunch, with strongly held beliefs. Many of them believe that to label their wines as organic would lump them in with what they regard as unreliable hippy-dippies (or, to put it another way, bad winemakers), and it is a brush with which they do not wish to be

tarred. So even if they farm totally in accordance with organic practice some producers refuse to let the certifying bodies come
anywhere near them.

There are other reasons for remaining uncertified. Maybe they
simply can't be bothered with all the paperwork, or with having
know-it-all inspectors snooping around their winery trying to teach
them to suck eggs. Some of the world's most expensive wines are
made according to organic or biodynamic principles without the
certification, and demand far exceeds supply for the fortunate
people making them. If you can get over £600 a *bottle* for your
wine, as the Domaine de la Romanée-Conti in Burgundy regularly
does, why bother to jump through the certifying hoops? At the top
level of winemaking, organic principles are very widely observed,
simply because the producers know their value. That in itself could
be said to be evidence enough for the advantages of being organic.

Another reason for refusing certification may be that the producers are fibbing about their organic status, and will sneak out into
the vineyard at dead of night to spray with something toxic if an
unexpected pest suddenly threatens to ravage the vines. So they
don't apply for certification because they know full well they'd fail
the test.

Simon Loftus, head of leading wine merchants Adnams and a
man known not to be a shrinking violet, says flatly that good
producers won't label their wines 'organic' because most organic
wine is bad. Polemic, certainly, but it's a point of view passionately
held by many winemakers.

I don't want to exclude from this book anyone who makes
terrific organic wine solely because they don't have certification. If
I only include wines certified by an official body, that means I can
at least be reasonably sure the wine is made organically. It doesn't,
on the other hand, ensure that the wine is any good. It's no guarantee of quality, only of provenance. So to make sure I include the
best wines available I have cast the net wider and included producers who make wine (or claim to) according to organic principles,
without having the certificate.

But it can be hard to discover who these winemakers are. Take Michel Chapoutier, for instance. He runs a large and well-known wine operation in France's Rhône valley, where he farms the family's own vineyard holdings and also acts as négociant, which means buying in grapes and wine from other growers and marketing them under his own name. The estates he farms himself are biodynamic; but not all the wines bought in are either organic or biodynamic. None of the wines bear any indication of organic status. So I asked him why not: what do consumers do who want to choose organic or biodynamic wines from his list?

Chapoutier explained that, historically, he hadn't wanted to label the wines organic because of the 'lazy dreamers of the 1960s'; the hippies who'd made such bad organic wine that the reputation of the stuff seemed sullied for ever. Now, however, mindful of the overall increase in competence among organic winemakers, and wanting to create a labelling structure to cater for quality as well as organic and biodynamic status, he has co-founded the certifying body Biodyvin along with such luminaries as Anne-Claude Leflaive, the legendary Burgundy winemaker of Domaine Leflaive, and Veronique Cochran from Château Falfas in Bordeaux. Beginning this year, we will start to see Biodyvin appearing on labels, which is a very welcome development. For now, the tasting notes in Chapter 9 will have to be the best guide to what is organic in the Chapoutier range.

The identification problem is widespread. Adnams once included in their wine list a note of producers who grew grapes according to organic principles but weren't certified. Loftus says he's not allowed to do that any more. 'The whole regulatory framework is complete nonsense, because you have to join organisations that have views irrelevant to you. They have a wider agenda, and joining implies commitment. So many great growers don't certify, and the organisations attract people for whom other aims are the first priority.'

So: to join the organic club, or not to join? I think the last word on this rests with Groucho Marx, the man who wouldn't join any club that would accept him as a member.

WHAT ARE WE GOING TO CALL THE UNCERTIFIED WINES?

Because the term 'organic' has legal status on a wine label, I need to make sure I stay on the right side of the Eurocrats while letting you know what's what. So we need a word to describe someone following organic principles but without the bit of paper to wave in the air.

The question is, what word? 'Natural'? Bit wishy-washy. 'Bio' is the word used in France and Germany to describe an organic wine. Which would be fine if, every time I used it, the word 'Baby' didn't creep irresistibly in front of it. 'Eco', on the other hand, is free of connotations – for me, anyway – and has the added advantage of being short. So 'eco' in the text will refer to any wine which claims to be produced according to organic principles but isn't certified.

In doing this I know I'm taking a great deal on trust. Is this wine-maker telling the truth when claiming to make eco wine? Should I instead be asking, as journalists are encouraged to do of politicians: 'Why is this bastard lying to me?' Consumers need to be aware that some unscrupulous growers claim organic status as just another way of jumping on a bandwagon.

CONVERSION

Becoming organic isn't something that happens overnight. A producer might wake up one morning and repent of all the chemicals they've sprayed on their patch over the last 20 years, and resolve in a flash to sin no more. But Damascene conversion in one's head is one thing – out on the land it's quite another. At least three years must elapse between the last use of conventional weapons and organic certification, three years during which the producer has to contend with vines weakened and distended from the use of chemicals but is unable to reach for the old combatants – the fungicides, herbicides and everything else they once relied on. It can be a tough time.

Robert Eden, winemaker at Comte Cathare in southern France, feels that EU and government grants available to winemakers wishing to convert to organic production should be more thoughtfully applied. People should be given grants to let the land lie fallow and recover for a year or three, and also to cover the cost of manure or green manure. 'The training element is totally missing. Certification isn't training, it's just people coming round looking at invoices' – the invoices that prove you've spent your grant on approved organic materials.

When winemakers convert to biodynamic viticulture, they have an immediate advantage over ordinary organic conversion. Using the homeopathic sprays recommended in biodynamics will immediately begin to strengthen and rejuvenate both the land and the vines, providing extra support right from the start to help the converting producer make the transition more easily. More on biodynamics in Chapter 6.

Rules and regulations: an example

Here's what one of the main German certifying bodies, the Federal Association for Ecological Viticulture e.v., lays down as the ground rules for organic cultivation:

- To maintain and improve vineyard soil fertility by means of appropriate cultivation measures, and to renounce and abstain from all measures which contravene this objective.
- To breed and grow healthy resistant vines without the application of herbicides, chemical synthetic insecticides and fungicides.
- To encourage and help propagate the diversity of plant and animal species within the vineyard ecosystem.
- To use raw materials and waste products of negligible toxicity to nature and to regenerate a largely uninterrupted production cycle.
- To reduce the concentration of certain critical elements in the vineyard soil and in water resources (such as nitrates, phosphates and vine protection additives).

- To renounce the cultivation of genetically manipulated plants.
- To create a secure existence on the basis of satisfying living conditions.

I especially like the last one – that's what it's all about, really. Why do it if you don't enjoy it?

BLACK AND WHITE OR SHADES OF GREY?

It's easy to imagine there are just two, mutually opposed choices in winemaking: conventional, which demands huge and indiscriminate chemical inputs, or organic, which works in harmony with the land, the vines and the seasons. But, of course, it isn't like that. It's not just black and white – there are shades of grey. It's analogue, a sliding scale, not on/off digital.

For instance, among the many producers who claim to farm organically, but aren't certified, there will be some whose reason for not certifying is that they reserve the right to spray as a last-ditch, backs-to-the-wall solution to pest infestation if the only alternative is to see the year's crop wither on the vine. Some might say this is a failure of nerve, and that if you've done everything in your power to strengthen the vine's natural resources, and used the various means of natural pest control available, you won't have any major problems. This is especially true of biodynamics, where the homeopathic sprays further bolster disease resistance and protection.

But what if, despite everything, you have a major threat to the crop? Do you stand by and let the pests have free run, or do you take action using non-organic methods? This is a question New Zealand organic grower James Millton of Millton Vineyard has faced. James encountered a severe problem with mealy bug infestation in six rows of vines in 1994. The only approved organic weapon against this pest was pyrethrum spray, which doesn't necessarily kill mealy bugs but does kill bees and other beneficial insects.

James decided instead to use a synthetic spray on those six rows of vines, both to kill off the mealy bugs and to ensure the survival of the insects working to protect the rest of his vines. As a result he stopped declaring his wines organic (though remaining organic and biodynamic in every other respect). He waited the three years it takes for conventional growers to convert to organic production, as a kind of 'reconversion' phase, and with the 1998 vintage he restored the organic designation to the wines.

I have never been faced with this kind of decision, and I can't imagine what it must be like to have to make it. The winemaker's livelihood is on the line at that point, and to a certain extent their ego too. The quality of the wine produced hooks right into a wine-maker's identity, reflecting personality and attitude to life in ways that maybe aren't immediately obvious to the producers them-selves.

And while I can empathise with the difficulties, I think consumers have the right to know what's going on in the vineyard from year to year in order to select a certain producer because of a commit-ment to organic principles. Maybe this means that only fully certified organic wines will fit the bill. What I want to bring to your awareness is the fact that it's a sliding scale (and a slippery one at that).

All the producers of eco wine mentioned in this book are giving us information we have to take on trust. Maybe what we should do is encourage them to take that last step wherever possible and commit to certification. They will only be able to do that finan-cially, however, when their wines can achieve such a financial premium that sales in the good years will give them a reserve to cushion the bad years when disease or insect infestation reduces the yield to less than 20 per cent of the norm. It takes courage to be prepared to stand by and watch that happen.

THREE NOT-QUITE-ORGANIC PATHS

1. LUTTE RAISONNÉE

Bubbling under full organic status lie several different initiatives which encourage producers to intervene with chemicals as little as possible. In France there's the 'lutte raisonnée' or 'rational struggle', which is a struggle against pests and disease rather than reason itself. Here again organic principles are followed up to the point where spraying becomes, as Champagne grower Jean-Baptiste Geoffroy put it, 'the ultimate solution'. To hear this man talk is to sense a huge commitment to the soil, to the vines and to the complete expression of both in the much-abused French concept of 'terroir', the sense of a wine coming from a certain place.

I've also come across the expression 'biodynamisme raisonnée' in southern France. This, alas, has nothing to do with any of the biodynamic principles you'll find explained in this book; it's really a vague term for being sort of, but not quite, organic. I think it's a completely misleading and inaccurate term and really shouldn't be used, but try telling the French that.

2. INTEGRATED PEST MANAGEMENT (IPM)

This is an interesting intermediate stage which sits somewhere between out-and-out organics and conventional trigger-happy spraying. IPM aims to keep all pest populations below a damaging level. It does this by monitoring the weather, pest life cycles and biology, local patterns and environmental conditions to create a picture of what is likely to happen when, and what the minimum intervention would be to deal with it.

IPM is a step forward from the conventional viticultural regime which involves spraying ten or more times a year, a timetable determined by the calendar – spray each month, regardless – rather than by what is actually happening in the vineyard.

IPM producers need to be very knowledgeable and aware of what's happening, keeping a close eye on exact pest levels. They constantly count both pests and predators: that way they'll know whether the pest population is being kept down below the danger level by the predators, or surging out of control.

In IPM the object is not to eradicate pests completely (which I think is all too often the aim in conventional grape growing) but to keep damage down to a tolerable level. In any case, it's not a beauty contest. Surface blemishes are acceptable on wine grapes – they're not intended for the table in that form, so no one will see them looking less than perfect.

Benzinger winery in Sonoma, California, provides a good example of the benefits of holding one's nerve. Its decision to tolerate pest damage was put to the test by an infestation of the destructive red spider mite during a heatwave. 'Mite populations began to rise, and so did visible damage,' explained manager Barry Sloane. 'Every day we were in the vineyard anxiously checking pest numbers, but we held off spraying because we felt the damage was cosmetic and not actually affecting vine health. Finally the weather cooled, mite populations dropped and we survived with only superficial damage – and without spraying once.'

Very often IPM-based growers will adopt other organic practices such as growing green manures in between the vine rows and planting the plum trees that harbour parasitic wasps, allowing a diverse range of life-forms to interact and do what comes naturally (eat each other). Often the hardest part for growers new to IPM is to unlearn the knee-jerk reaction of spraying at the first sight of a pest, and holding their fire until they believe intervention has become unavoidable.

IPM is clearly a step in the right direction, away from the habit of spraying and towards a more sensitive approach to the ecology of the vineyard. But the key to true organic viticulture is to look away from what you don't want – pests, bugs, fighting off insect infestations – and towards what you do want – a healthy vineyard that will have the strength in and of itself to ward off such pests. As John Williams of Californian organic estate Frog's Leap put it: 'The most effective control is to strengthen the vine. If you feed the soil, you feed the vine.'

3. INTEGRATED PRODUCTION OF WINE (IPW)

Used only in South Africa, this initiative was launched in June 1998 and by March 1999 it was claimed that more than 99 per cent of the total wine production in South Africa was committed to this process. Organisers claim that because the guidelines cover all aspects of production, from the vineyard to the final bottled product, IPW makes South Africa a leader in this field. Signing up to it is voluntary but having signed, producers are legally bound to follow all ordinances. The 1999 harvest will be their first big test, so you'll see some form of words about IPW on labels or some sort of marketing campaign from the 2000 vintage onwards.

So, looking at the densely typed regulations in detail, what do we find? Adherence to IPM, for a start, which is a good sign. And sulphur levels are held reasonably low too, close to those for organic wine, which is also a good sign – no disguising bad wine-making with heavy doses of sulphur.

Individual wineries in other countries try to do things along similar lines. Mondavi, the big California producer, has a 'sustainable' policy it has followed for over 20 years on over 405 hectares (1000 acres) in Napa Valley. Admittedly there are some weasel words here. They use alternatives to chemicals 'wherever possible', and 'most vineyards exceed many standards set by California Certified Organic Farmers' (yes, yes, what about the standards they *don't* meet?). Nevertheless, they're replacing herbicides with ploughing, encouraging natural predators, using cover crops. This is all good stuff, and a world away from the gung-ho 'prepare-to-repel-boarders' attitude of those whose first instinct is to reach for the spray gun. E&J Gallo is also subscribing to many of these methods in its Russian River vineyards in Sonoma. There are encouraging signs that large organisations will follow organic principles where it makes good economic or ecological sense.

The key thing is, it really isn't all cut and dried in the organic wine world. It's a bit like the German Green Party used to be, with the Fundis – who took a totally fundamentalist line on everything and were practically back to the horse and cart – versus the Realos, who wanted to work in the real world, whatever that is. As you can imagine, they argued a lot. I think it depends greatly on your own view of the world. You'll either take a fundamentalist line – certified wines or nothing – or you'll look at wines of varying shades of grey and make up your own mind on what constitutes a healthy, ecologically sound wine.

My whole point is that people deserve a choice. Sometimes we want to buy organic but there is no certified organic wine available, so what do we do? With this information we can at least make enlightened choices about the wine we buy.

3
ORGANIC WINE VERSUS CONVENTIONAL WINE IN THE VINEYARD

GRAPES AND FARMING METHODS

IN ORDER TO understand what makes organic wine different, we need to look in some detail at how grapes are grown and wine is made. As we go through each of the processes in turn, we can look at the problems and challenges that arise, how conventional practice deals with them, and what organic growers do instead of spraying with noxious chemicals.

To help with this, I've called upon two very different organic producers, James Millton of Millton Vineyard in New Zealand and Richard Doughty of Château Richard in Bergerac, France, to comment on the various practices and their attitudes to them. Both make really good wine, but each has a different take on what works, formulated after many years' experience of farming his particular patch. The gap between their viewpoints reflects the difficulty anyone mad enough to try to present a unified view of organic viticulture would encounter.

One of the key principles of organic farming is crop rotation – growing each type of crop, brassicas, roots, whatever, in a different patch of ground each year so the pests that delight in destroying one type of crop are disappointed the following year by the arrival of, for example, spuds instead of Brussels sprouts. But, of course, you can't do that in a vineyard. Vines take four years to establish and then a good few years more before they reach full production. (After that, they can go on for 40 years or more, maybe even up to a century, giving fewer grapes but of better quality. See? Youth isn't everything.) So organic winemakers have to take many different steps to avoid the ravages of pestilence.

Winemaker profile:
James Millton, Millton Vineyard, Poverty Bay, New Zealand

James Millton's experiments with fermentation began early, as a result of which he was expelled from school. Those blackberries were for making jam, not wine, a fact he learned the hard way. Entering the wine trade he trained at Yalumba in Australia's Barossa Valley, Bollinger in Champagne and Château Palmer in Bordeaux, marrying fellow Kiwi, Annie, on the way.

After two vintages in the Rhine valley James came back to New Zealand and took a job managing his father-in-law's vines. But, after a couple of vintages together, family differences started to show as James and Annie's commitment to organic production grew increasingly at odds with her father's use of chemicals. Eventually they leased the vineyards from Annie's parents, and initiated a full organic conversion programme. James's was the first certified winery in New Zealand.

James and Annie's winery stands beside the Te Arai river, where settlers had planted vines as early as 1871. The siting of the vineyards isn't exactly hospitable. The climate is mild, so insect pests aren't killed off by cold over winter. It is damp, so mildew and fungus threaten summer success. Fertile soil encourages rampant leaf growth and there's a biting prevailing north-west wind. Nevertheless, dedicated application of biodynamic principles has helped overcome these problems. You won't see a certification symbol on their labels, though, because New Zealand's biodynamic certifying

---

body doesn't approve of the consumption of alcohol and therefore won't certify wine.

'After 12 years of growing biodynamically, pests and diseases are not problems but merely indicators that some aspects are out of balance. More importantly, for myself really, the work is a pleasure, I enjoy it and so I do not look at things as problems, maybe challenges! After all these years we are getting confident with our organic inputs, so much so that orthodox growers are asking for advice on "controlling" several diseases.'

I asked James what he felt he did differently to conventional winemakers. 'We have five senses and these can be taught us. Most important is the sixth sense which is actually sensitivity; and then there is common sense. We cannot be taught those and it is only experience from using the other five senses that will enable the other two to come more clearly.'

THE ANSWER LIES IN THE SOIL ...

Organic producers of any crop focus on the soil as the bedrock of fertility – especially the biodynamic growers, who view the soil as a living organism and aim for harmony between it, themselves, and the cosmos. Such attitudes function in completely the opposite way to those of conventional viticulture, where the farmer focuses on the vine not the soil. In intensive grape growing the soil is viewed as something inert, unable to sustain productivity on its own, demanding benevolent human intervention.

So the intensive farmer zooms around in a cloud of herbicide and insecticide to stop all those nasty bugs and weeds helping themselves to the nutrients that rightly belong to the chosen plants alone. And, of course, these sprays kill off all the natural bacteria that create soil fertility in the first place, so the grower has to recreate that fertility artificially with chemical fertilisers. These artificially created nutrients, being water-soluble, are mostly washed away or absorbed by weeds – so you need even more fertiliser to replace what's lost after rainfall. The excess nitrogen from these fertilisers causes the vine to grow faster and taller than it would under normal, balanced conditions. This distends and weakens the vine's cell structure, making it vulnerable to attack from disease and parasites.

This means you have to spray against pests and diseases. Sure, you kill the pests with these poisons, but you also kill the predators that naturally prey on the pests. Fungicides will not only destroy the fungus attacking the plant – botrytis (grey rot), say – but also all the bacteria and yeasts the vine actually needs to maintain its internal balance.

The chemical residues that fall between the vines mix with rainwater and penetrate deep into the soil, and gradually sterilise it. All those micro-organisms, bacteria, insects, larvae – everything that gives the soil life and vitality – gone. Great swathes of soil in the world's finest winemaking areas, such as Bordeaux and Burgundy, are dead. Too many years of intensive spraying have turned once-living soils into inert matter. Some say that the reason wines from Chile, for example, are lively, fresh and exciting is that the vineyards are relatively new and haven't been poisoned to death yet. But they're probably working on it, just like the rest of the world is.

Winemaker profile:
Richard Doughty, Château Richard, Bergerac, France

Richard Doughty has an English father and French mother, and is equally at home in both languages – helpful when dealing with the local wine committee of which he was recently president. He started his working life closely involved with a different liquid – oil, via offshore exploration engineering – but a broken leg cast him ashore with time to think and he abandoned oil in favour of wine in the late 1980s. He rapidly embraced organic principles, and sees his

---

progression in winemaking as a progressive willingness to throw away the rulebook and listen to what the vines actually tell him.

For instance, his wines are noticeably lower in acidity than those of his neighbours. This makes them very well balanced and attractive. According to Richard, this acidity balance is simply what the vines produce. If that's what they want to do, he says, who is he to intervene?

The green manure between the vines grows randomly – this year, lamb's lettuce appeared. 'I can get very high-quality, nitrate-free salads just by bending down in the vines. I have just seen my parents brave the cheerful January sunshine on this mild day to go on a picking expedition.

'While the vines are sleeping these plants are perfectly welcome to grow, but sometime in late spring they will become less desirable so some plough or other device will come and disturb and probably bury them.'

Richard farms organically but dislikes putting it on the label because of the connotations the French make with 'laboratories and white coats'. He has also incorporated some biodynamic principles, but refuses to take it all on board. 'I believe more in plants than people. And more in practical down-to-earth reality than in "faith". I'm a pretty philosophical type but religious faith and dogma leave me "chilly".'

He is, however, strongly of the opinion that vines have personality, and that each variety and each individual plant in its own soil will behave differently. He teased me with horoscopes for vine varieties: 'I like the almost Aries character of a Merlot, a willing but naïve and impetuous plant compared with the earthy Taurean Cabernet Franc ... I could speak for hours about the living "personality" of vine varieties. Vines really are likeable friends to live with. You're nice to them and they're nice to you.'

A SPIRAL OF DEPENDENCE

The persistent round of trying to cover up the last mistake with yet more chemicals creates a spiral of problems. Entering a vicious circle like this creates a deepening dependence on chemicals – a dependence felt by both plant and grower. The plant because it grows weak, lowers its resistance to bugs and disease, and needs to be propped up by sprays and chemicals. The grower because all these chemicals force him or her to dig ever deeper into shallow pockets to pay for the chemicals, which means even more intensive farming, wringing out every last bunch of grapes from the vine, in order to pay for the products the vines have become dependent on. The chemicals get stronger and stronger, as the bugs become more resistant, so protective clothing must be worn to spray the grapes – grapes whose juice we'll be consuming.

And if you think this cycle of dependence is harmful, what about the genetically modified dependency spiral? When plants have been engineered to resist the herbicides that will kill off all the surrounding weeds, the farmer is forced into paying whatever the genetic engineering companies demand as the price for keeping the GM plants alive.

Focusing on the soil instead as the source of fertility and strength boosts the vines' natural resistance to pests and diseases. The organic farmer then supplements this with a series of non-chemical methods for fighting off all the pests and predators that plague the vineyard.

IRRIGATION – IS IT OK TO WATER THE VINES?

Sometimes I think there's a hint of sadism with some growers, who explain with glee that the reason they appear to neglect their vines is that the vine thrives on stress. Stress in this case being caused not by workaholism but by lack of water and nutrients.

If you've ever been to wine country, you'll know that the best vines aren't usually planted in fertile valleys but on hillside slopes, in poor soil, often apparently into bare rock. Too fertile a soil, with nutrients near the surface, will mean the vine's roots won't bother going down very far. Deep roots encourage the vine to take in flavourful trace minerals and seek out water deep underground – resulting in stronger, healthier plants and, of more interest to us, increased concentration of flavour in the grape.

This doesn't happen with chemical fertilisers. There you're feeding the roots directly, through water, with water-soluble nutrients. It may seem like a short cut, but roots pampered this way will see no reason to burrow down deep into the soil to find the food they need – and they'll suffer as a result. Too close to the surface means they'll be less likely to be able to nourish themselves in a drought – and in most of Europe irrigation of vines is banned, except for young vines struggling to establish themselves. (And if the cynical among us are enquiring how often this ban is flouted, I for one couldn't possibly comment.)

In many parts of the New World, though, irrigation is a necessary part of grape growing, and there the key questions become those of optimum water levels and the best means of administering it – sprinklers or drip feeders, for instance. For organic growers another key question is the quality, and source, of the water being pumped into the vineyard. Organic guidelines in Canada, for instance, require water quality to be tested every five years.

Growers who irrigate can more readily control the amount of water stress the vines suffer. Not enough water and leaves will drop, followed by decreasing berry size and juice volume. Too much water and vines will have vibrantly green leaves and huge clusters of berries, but of poorer quality. The grapes will take longer to ripen and have high acids and low sugars, and not much in the way of varietal character. After all, we do want the grape to taste of something.

Too much water, or too many bunches of grapes on the vine, leads to what the French delightfully call 'faire pisser les vignes' – nothing to do with that description, beloved of wine writers, of Sauvignon Blanc smelling like cats' pee. Grapes bloated with water

A *success story*

John Williams of Frog's Leap vineyard in California bought a parcel of vines which he knew were terminally infected with phylloxera, a louse that attacks vine roots so they become unable to draw up moisture and subsequently die. He reckoned he had the chance to get maybe one or two last harvests out of the vines before grubbing them up and finding the money to replant with resistant vines.

As he tells it: 'I talked to the vines and made a deal with them. I'll give you the soil you need to store water, and I'll cut off your irrigation.' He immediately sowed green manure and ripped out the irrigation pipes. His neighbour, by contrast, from whom he had bought the patch, irrigated and used herbicide regularly. Green manure, when ploughed in immediately, adds organic matter and builds microbial activity which creates soil structure. Such soil soaks up rain like a sponge, so there's no need to irrigate. Winter rain seeps deep into the newly open-textured ground, unlike the neighbour's patch which, deadened by long use of herbicide, was so compacted you couldn't get a spade into it and water sat in sheets on the surface, unable to seep down.

The roots on John's vines plunged deeper underground, to over 30 m (100 ft) – and overcame phylloxera to thrive still today. His neighbour, on the other hand, had to grub up his vines because the infestation became overwhelming, and, when they were dug up John saw that the irrigated roots stretched down less than 30 cm (12 in). The first year, John cut the grapes off the vines just as they were forming, to give the vines a chance to recover. The next year, yields from that vineyard increased by over a ton per acre.

will give you plenty of liquid but precious little flavour. For a quality-conscious producer, quantity is not what it's about.

Many organic producers do everything they can to force the vine roots deep down into the subsoil to look for water, absorbing trace elements and minerals on their way. Some will plough between the vines from time to time. This cuts off any vine roots too close to the surface, forcing the roots deeper underground. Loosening the soil around the vines also stops it becoming too compacted, which prevents water and nutrients getting deep down into the soil.

WEEDS – THE ORGANIC GROWER'S FRIENDS

Then there's the comforting habit of letting weeds grow between the vines. If ever you needed an excuse for not getting the hoe out, this is it. Some people call weeds 'volunteers', and point out that they were there first, and they do have a point. You can do one of two things to deal with weeds: grow green manures, or just give them their head. Some weeds are very useful. Dock, for instance, helps combat powdery mildew, scourge of damp climates, and its deep taproot helps break up compacted soil.

Green manures are crops of plants such as clover or rye. They are grown for many purposes. They are 'companion crops', put there to complement the needs of the vines. They can fix essential elements in the soil, like nitrogen – with the added advantage that nitrogen formed this way can't be washed away so easily. They bring in natural predators to attack many vineyard pests, restoring a natural balance. Then, at the end of their life cycle, the green manures are ploughed in, adding organic matter to the soil. All in all a very Good Thing. Looks lovely, too. Cover crops also encourage spiders, which are voracious predators, as anyone who's watched a spider at work in their garden will know.

Once upon a time, the control freaks in the grape-growing fraternity would operate a scorched earth policy between the vines. Sometimes they plough (which does have the advantage of easing compaction and forcing vine roots to dig down further) and sometimes they apply herbicides. The Germans were particularly keen on keeping things neat.

But now even they've realised the benefits of growing greenstuff, even if it's only along every other row. At least then you have something to walk along when pruning or picking without disappearing up to your ankles in mud.

Some growers – even some organic ones – use flame-throwers to burn weeds off, though others point out that this simply substitutes petrochemicals for herbicides. Even if you're not poisoning the ground with the flame fuel you *are* using up natural resources, so from an overall ecological perspective that isn't a great idea.

VINE FOOD: ANIMAL, VEGETABLE OR MINERAL

Vegetable and animal manures are prized by the organic grape grower. Vegetation not ploughed in directly is composted, which allows it to break down at a high enough temperature (around 60°C/100°F) to kill off weed seeds and any lurking pathogens – especially important if composting manure from livestock not raised organically.

Four key minerals for vines are nitrogen, phosphorus, potassium and magnesium. Nitrogen you get through green manures; phosphorus and potassium are best introduced through composted farmyard manures. Magnesium comes from natural lime or bone meal (not a welcome thought for vegetarians). And for other trace elements, many vineyards are sprayed with seaweed – this apparently contains not only the minerals the vines need but also hormones promoting growth and health.

How often to apply all these? Reading the weeds can tell you a lot. Different weeds thrive in different soil conditions; for instance, vetch grows in low fertility soils, while dandelions and docks thrive in acid, heavy soils. This reading of crops has a long history. In Bordeaux the habit of planting rose bushes at the end of each row of vines wasn't so the labourers would make time to relax, stop and smell the flowers. This was a hard-nosed early warning system to alert growers to the presence of mildew.

Good growers will apply all these nutrients little and often; overdoing it causes all kinds of trouble. Add too much nitrogen, for instance, and you'll get fabulous, luxuriant vine leaves but very small bunches of grapes – or the fruit may not set at all.

PESTS AND DISEASES

Damp, the British scourge, is a major enemy of grape growers in all cooler climates. Not a major problem in the south of France but a serious hindrance further north in the Loire, say, or in New Zealand. Fungal diseases are caused by damp conditions, and weeds can also make things worse by increasing humidity. A hot, dry climate – Mediterranean – is ideal for growing grapes without chemical intervention, which is one reason why the south of France has so many organic growers. But it seems to me that motivation is the key factor, not climate, and you'll find organic producers in much less auspicious climates battling heroically to produce wine according to what they believe rather than doing what's easiest.

Planting a vineyard from scratch means many decisions can be made that will make life easier. Some grape varieties respond better to organic growing than others. Good drainage helps, and so does the method of training the vines. Vines are by nature undisciplined creatures; left to themselves they flop and sprawl, looking for a tree to climb up, and the serried ranks of immaculately neat vines stretching across the hillside are the result of somebody's backbreaking work. The ideal shape for the growing vine will allow lots of light and air to get in. Light for ripening; air to stop damp creeping in and with it mildew and fungus. This is what the arcane-sounding practice of 'canopy management' is all about; canopy is just a posh term for the leaf cover the vines develop each year.

Viruses plague the vineyard and are carried by insects, so tools must be kept scrupulously clean to fight the pests. One piece of research suggests that marigolds can help suppress the nematode worm, small scourge of vine roots. That'll bring some welcome colour if it catches on.

FUNGUS – A BOGEYMAN

Fungal disease is one of the worst problems affecting organic growers, because they can't have recourse to fungicidal sprays. And it doesn't matter if your climate is cool and damp or hot and humid: each has a fungal devastation to match – downy and powdery mildew (*aka* oidium) respectively. Then there's botrytis, or grey rot, only too familiar to gardeners. If you want to make rich, sweet white wine such as Sauternes then botrytis is desirable, as its fungal fingers pierce the grape and allow the water in the juice to evaporate, concentrating the sugar left behind. If, on the other hand, sweet whites are not on the agenda, botrytis is a disaster.

So what to do? Prevention is better than cure: keep nitrogen low to avoid creating lush soft growth that won't withstand fungus attacks. Spray with seaweed to encourage strong growth. Garlic wards off fungus as well as vampires. And copper-based sprays – such as the famous Bordeaux mixture – will also act as preventatives, as will sulphur.

However nothing is without its consequences. Sulphur and copper don't persist in the plant so the treatment needs to be repeated every couple of weeks or so. And copper build-up in the soil is undesirable because it's toxic and it stunts vine growth. This is now a problem in Bordeaux after a century or more of applying the mixture. Here again, however, the organic approach makes amends: plenty of humus and lime will neutralise a copper overdose. The best organic defence against botrytis is thinning out the leaf canopy to allow plenty of air to circulate, as the conventional sprays are non-organic and can't be used.

Then there's 'dead-arm disease', which has results you can guess at and which is caused by the fungus entering the vine through a wound, such as when pruning. Organic growers fight this by pruning late, after rain, when sap flow is more vigorous; or they paint the wound with sulphur.

A lot of preventative work in the organic vineyard is simply common sense; keeping things clean, removing any diseased or dying bits of vine, boosting the vine's own resources and introducing predators. Pheromone traps are based on sex, aimed at confusing male bugs by simulating the smell of the female so they move towards the trap instead of finding a female and mating (must remember that one). Parasitic wasps will prey on vineyard pests and can be encouraged by planting plum trees, their preferred habitat, around the vineyards as Fetzer does in California.

PESTICIDES: DEATH BY SPRAY GUN

Pesticides ... the key weapons in the arsenal of the conventional grower. Be they fungicides, bactericides, insecticides, nematicides, miticides, these are the chemicals to have at the ready to prevent the pests gaining the upper hand. Because, of course, you can't leave nature to find its own balance, can you?

First of all, let's look at what a pesticide actually is. Each one consists of an active ingredient, usually bearing a long Latin name, which is mixed with other ingredients such as wetting agents. These are what allows the product to be sprayed. Sometimes two or more active ingredients are mixed together; sometimes this leads to incompatibility, so the grower needs to have a good understanding of chemistry even before donning the protective clothing.

These active ingredients are toxic. How could they not be? They deal death to whatever is causing trouble in the vineyard, so it's not surprising that they'll also deal death to anything that stands in their way, from beneficial insects that might otherwise have lunched on the pest, to the humans who unwittingly breathe in the spray. There are well-documented studies demonstrating the health risks to farm and vineyard workers using chemicals on the land, but passers-by and neighbouring inhabitants also suffer. In California there is considerable concern about schoolchildren inhaling pesticides sprayed on vineyards near to their schools.

The pressure group Californians for Pesticide Reform points to the use of a total of 17 different insecticides, herbicides and fumigants in wine production, many of which contain possible carcinogens. In California alone, 59 million lb of pesticides were used on wine grapes in 1995. And, by an extraordinary coincidence, grape production accounts for one-third of all pesticide-associated illness in the state. Illnesses such as contact dermatitis, a skin inflammation reported by vineyard workers at a rate ten times higher than other agricultural workers.

DANGERS TO WINE DRINKERS FROM CHEMICALS

Problems arise for both workers and wine drinkers when pesticides are stored in the body's tissues and accumulate over time. This can sometimes explain the headaches that are usually put down to over-indulgence.

Exposure to toxic chemicals can come at us from many angles. In Australia, grape growers have been warned about the dangers of burning Permapine posts. These wooden posts, used for supporting vines, are treated with copper chrome arsenate which is released into the atmosphere when burnt. In 1997 four people were hospitalised in Victoria after using Permapine wood on their barbecue. It's illegal to burn this wood in Australia, but, despite containing these heavy metals, it's not illegal to use it in stakes because the metals are embedded in the wood and only released by burning. Apparently it's quite OK to dispose of these posts in landfill sites. No possible danger of the metals leaching out of the wood over time, obviously ...

Another problem with dangerous chemicals leaching out of wood recently came to light in Bordeaux. In December 1998 *The Guardian* reported that Bordeaux grapegrowers had admitted a cover-up. Thousands of bottles of wine, around 1 per cent of all bottles of Bordeaux wine produced in the previous two years, had been contaminated with an illegal pesticide, chlorophenol. This pesticide, applied to barrels and wooden buildings, had been banned in the EU since 1991, but the cause of the Bordeaux contamination was not subsequently identified until 1993. According to *The Guardian*, the Bordeaux Wine Board's spokeswoman, Sophie Girard, said the public had not been informed because it was a 'relatively minor problem'. Oh, thanks.

The contamination was hard to spot because it smells very similar to cork taint. The chemist who originally pinpointed the cause of the contamination, Pascal Chatonnet, was quoted as saying that the wood in half of Bordeaux's barrels was still affected.

It can be hard enough taking back a wine because you believe there's something wrong with it. But if the contamination may have been caused by noxious chemicals it's high time we started speaking up about wine that tastes odd, off, or in any way unusual. And, of course, minimise the risks to our health by selecting organic wines.

Keeping the vineyard pure

There is also the problem of cross-contamination, most often a problem when there are lots of small parcels of vines next to one another. What do you do when your neighbour's spray goes a bit wide and hits your crop? This is a particular problem in the Mosel valley in Germany, where organic producers farm cheek-by-jowl with chemical-based neighbours. The vineyards of the Mosel are vertiginous. To make life easier, many conventional growers hire helicopters to spray the vineyards. Now if you're farming organically on one of these tiny hillside parcels and your vines are just a yard or two from the ones the helicopter is aiming for, it doesn't bode well, does it?

The cost of giving up chemicals

Bob Blue, winemaker with Fetzer in California, acknowledges that some conventional weeding practices are hard to turn away from at first and that start-up costs can be high for converting to organics. 'You have to sell some machinery, like your spray rigs, and buy some new kit. You're looking at maybe $100,000 for equipment change.' (But of course smaller vineyards can pool resources and share kit.) It's labour-intensive – young vines need to be hand-hoed to knock out the weed competition – but you can keep costs down, he says, by not needing your vineyard to look too beautiful. 'You can spend $150 an acre on weed control, but that's more for aesthetic pleasure and to knock out the competition. If things don't have to look perfect it need only cost you $50 an acre.'

There's a lot of truth in this. If you've had neatness drilled into you from an early age, how easy is it to let go of that and tolerate weed growth? How much money does it cost to keep things looking neat? Much better if you can sit back and be relaxed about the weeds, but that's not always straightforward for some people.

Harvesting the grapes

In the organic world, producers tend to play a long game, longer than many growers of intensively produced grapes. They have to. They need to monitor vineyard activity much more closely because they can't – won't – rush in with a spray gun wielding instant death at the first sign of an insect pest. And they'll wait to harvest at the optimum moment. This may mean risking rain in the attempt to time the maturity of the grapes just right, rather than follow the path of conventional producers who play safe and rush out to drag the crop indoors to the safety of the fermenting vat at the first opportunity.

Once upon a time, harvesting was simple: assemble a team of pickers, train them to discard unripe or diseased bunches, choose the right moment for optimum ripeness (avoid rain – water on the grapes will dilute the wine), and away you go. Oh, and have an army of caterers on hand to feed this ravenous team, because they could be around for three weeks or more until all the crop is safely gathered in.

43

It doesn't all have to happen at once, because not all vineyards are ready to pick at exactly the same moment. If several varieties are grown, such as the Bordeaux combo of Cabernet Sauvignon, Franc and Merlot, they normally won't all ripen at once, so they can conveniently be harvested in neat succession.

HOW BEST TO HARVEST: UPRIGHT PICKING TEAMS VERSUS HORIZONTAL SLAPPERS

But suppose there's an optimum point of ripeness, when the balance of sugar (which increases with ripening) and acidity (which decreases with ripening) is exactly right? The grapes won't hang around, frozen at the perfect balance, waiting for the pickers to spend a week reaching all four corners of the vineyard. In a hot climate there will be a significant difference between the sugar concentration at the beginning and the end of a single day, never mind a week.

These days there's an alternative to ravenous hordes of pickers: harvesting machines. These odd-looking monsters, usually painted pale blue, are a common sight in vineyard landscapes these days. I still think of them as automatic milking machines, which is silly, but the name has stuck in my head and won't be dislodged even by the horizontal slapper, which is the irresistible name given to the currently favoured machines. These use fibreglass rods to strike the vine foliage and dislodge the fruit, which comes away either as single berries or as whole bunches. And the fans of mechanical harvesters say: use a machine and race up the rows in minutes, not days. Pick your moment and then pick your grapes. Simple.

Some berries will be damaged, and many will be punctured; so juice will escape and begin to oxidise as soon as it makes contact with the air. To prevent this, producers use sulphur dioxide, but organic producers want to minimise sulphur use. Harvesting at night or at dawn helps, because it means the grapes don't arrive at the winery overheated. In hot climates, midday harvesting can mean the grapes arrive at the winery heated to 40°C/104°F. Would you want your grapes to be processed as non-colourfast cottons? I think not.

Two views on mechanical harvesting machines

In favour, James Millton

'You don't have to feed them, pay them for holidays, social and other taxes and they are just as happy working at 5 o'clock in the morning at 5°C so you don't need to use sulphur dioxide in the winery to prevent oxidation.

'Hand-harvesting leaves grapes out in the sun and they get warm. Machine-harvesting depends on the set-up of the machine by the operator to make it the most effective. So what do we do? Both. If inclement weather is forecast, we can leave harvesting until the last minute and then pick. We pick our hillside vineyards by hand.'

Against, Richard Doughty

'Of course picking machines are allowed in organic farming – they are mechanical and don't add anything non-organic to the juice. They do add whatever was on the leaves, for example, rainwater or dew if leaves were wet, lizards, snails, occasionally a tree-climbing grass snake, insects, leaves, staples, bark etc. They break the grape skins. They are noisy and unfriendly, never laugh and will work all night, therefore the person receiving the grapes has to work at their rhythm not the human pickers' rhythm.

'If you take the trouble to tell your pickers: "I don't want you to pick the nasty looking or smelling grapes", in most cases they don't pick them, whereas you can spend hours trying to adjust the machines. They are plain daft and shake the grapes off the vine whether or not they are on a nice bunch or a less nice bunch.

'The machines are heavy and crush the soil structure. If you've got your own you can use it when you like, but, if shared, you have to fit in with the others. But they are cheaper than French salaries ...'

The other issue relating to automatic milkers is the environmental damage they cause. Trundling that weight of machinery up and down the rows of vines compacts the soil and undoes a lot of the careful work done earlier in the season to loosen it up.

HOW ORGANICS BEGAN

By this time you'd be forgiven for wondering how we got into this mess in the first place. Having seen the destructive, vicious circle conventional growers can get themselves into, how on earth did we let this ever come about? It's as if there must once have been some romantic golden age of agriculture – think The Haywain, think Laurie Lee – when we all farmed in harmony with the nature, close to the changing seasons.

Er ... not quite. Nutrition was a rather hit-and-miss affair in Western Europe for thousands of years. So was grape growing. Soil fertility was not a concept much understood in the last few millennia, and as a result millions died of starvation.

Neolithic farmers arriving here from the Mediterranean around 3500 BC started it – felling woodland to create fields for crops and livestock. In just a few hundred years they'd created a land so degraded it could barely support sheep. Denuded of the protective mantle of trees and grass, the earth simply eroded. Five thousand years on, we haven't learned much. Worldwide, we lose around 25 million tons of topsoil from vineyards and farmland every single year.

Lack of fodder to overwinter animals meant that most were slaughtered before winter came so there was little manure. Soil fertility declined inexorably, and a series of disastrous famines set the scene for the Black Death in 1348. A third, maybe a half of the entire UK population died.

Scarcer labour meant that once-cultivated land returned to grass, and sheep farming, which was much less labour intensive, grew in popularity. Profitable export trade in wool encouraged greedy landowners – feudal lords and the Catholic church – to confiscate common land, and the inhabitants of maybe two thousand villages were forcibly evicted to make way for vast sheep walks. In the fourteenth and fifteenth centuries sheep outnumbered humans by four to one. (Sounds a bit like Cumbria today. Except on bank holidays, of course.)

A century of quiet resting under grass and sheep manure did the trick; slowly soil fertility returned. Rapid population growth – tripling in the nineteenth century – and the migration of dispossessed peasants to the cities to labour under the industrial revolution created a very profitable trade in supplying food to the expanding landless workforce. Market gardens sprang up on the edges of cities, many using the intensive bed system developed by Parisian vegetable growers who were fuelled by the huge amounts of manure generated by the city's horse-drawn transport system. Fears that demand would outstrip supply were salved by the importation of grain and meat from the colonies. Their lower costs forced British prices down by a quarter and many farmers went bankrupt. And nearly two million acres of wheat returned to grass, again.

This is when the warning bells first began ringing – over a century ago. Fertility of soils in long-term cultivation declined measurably. Thousands of peasants from Britain and Europe emigrated to America because their own land could no longer support them.

Science finally came up with an answer. The 'father of agricultural chemistry', Justus von Liebig, discovered which chemical substances plants needed from the soil and how these substances were absorbed. One key discovery was plants' need for nitrogen – but where to find it? Air is nearly 80 per cent nitrogen but that doesn't help the plants. Only clovers and their relations can 'fix' nitrogen from the air into the soil where it can be of use to other plants. Animal manure contains a small amount of nitrogen and up to now that had been the main source, but demand now outstripped supply and attempts were made to import guano (sea fowl dung) from Chile to help out, a material viewed with suspicion by British farmers. (None of that foreign muck, thank you.)

Fast forward to 1914 and the frantic research and technological advancement that accompanies an outbreak of war. Three key wartime discoveries affected agriculture:

- Extracting nitrogen from the atmosphere to make explosives led to the development of nitrogen-based fertilisers.
- The technology for building tanks became the technology for building tractors (swords into ploughshares, anyone?).
- Poison gases used in trench warfare formed the basis for insecticides.

As chemical-based agriculture developed after the war so did awareness of the need for a different approach. In 1924 the essential elements of the system that came to be known as biodynamics were first applied in Germany (see Chapter 6).

Despite advances in chemical agriculture, the majority of Britain's food was imported right up until 1939. When the German U-boats cut British supply lines early in World War II a vulnerable government exhorted the population to 'Dig for Victory', and every available patch of land was ploughed up and planted.

To repair the devastation caused by that war, huge post-war investment poured into Europe via the Marshall Plan and industry was rebuilt. Land labour departed to the cities for more lucrative factory work and agriculture came to be seen as just another industrial process. Increased mechanisation and specialisation was supported by government grants, maximising food production by intensive use of chemical fertilisers and pesticides. Machines demand large, straight fields, so hedgerows were grubbed up to create the prairies we see today. Farmers received fertiliser subsidies, and grants to turn wild natural habitats such as marshland and heathland into yet more fields.

Joining what is now the European Union in 1973 came with a guarantee to farmers that the state would buy any food they could not sell. Guess what? Output soared, and the problem became one of disposing of vast wine lakes and wheat mountains – at a cost of over £20 billion a year.

It's not only surplus wine and food that now burden us, but surplus chemical residues left to pollute the earth and water. We've become increasingly concerned about the environmental damage caused by chemical-based agriculture – nitrates from fertiliser run-off poisoning water supplies, pesticides poisoning wildlife, the destruction of 150,000 miles of hedgerows to create vast prairie fields, destroying wildlife habitats.

No wonder soil erosion is still such a problem. Some experts believe that almost half of Britain's arable land is at risk. Populations of some common birds – songthrush, bullfinch – have dropped by half since 1970. And the soil is starving – degraded, denied organic matter, and continuously cropped.

So, several thousand years on, we have infinitely more knowledge, but it would seem we're no better at creating a fertile soil than the Neoliths were. Unless, of course, you farm organically. Organic farming seems to hold the key to sustainable food and drink, but at present it costs more – partly because the government persists in subsidising intensive chemical-based farming at the expense of organic farming, and partly because the true costs of intensive farming are not reflected in the cost of the food. Who pays for removing the fertilisers and other poisons from the water supply? The water companies. Which means all of us, whether or not we eat chemically produced food and drink. Add those costs to the price of intensively farmed food, and strip out the subsidies, and the picture would be very, very different.

4
WINERY WIZARDRY:
TECHNIQUES THAT SEPARATE ORGANIC AND CONVENTIONAL WINEMAKERS

IT'S IN THE wine cellar that producers make or break a wine, though wines can still only be as good as their raw ingredients. You can make a bad wine from good grapes (and believe me, many do) but you can't very well make a good wine from bad grapes.

Here again, organic winemakers tend to do things differently. The single biggest difference is that they use much less sulphur than most conventional winemakers. Sulphur is the major cause of headaches the morning after a bottle of wine (unless, of course, you were on a multi-bottle bender, in which case you don't need me to tell you what happened). Organic winemaking demands much lower levels of sulphur than conventional winemaking allows, which is a great comfort to asthmatics and those with sulphur sensitivity, and also more pleasant for the rest of us. (For more on sulphur, see pages 52–55.)

Although organic grape growing is strictly controlled and monitored, there is less regulation in the winery – apart from maximum permitted sulphur levels, of course. What marks out good winemaking practice in general could be summed up as 'minimum intervention': letting the grapes turn into wine as naturally as possible; mucking about with the product in all its stages as little as possible. Obviously this demands skill, knowledge and nerve – the courage to let the emerging wine evolve in the way it wants to, rather than how the winemaker thinks it ought to be. Speaking to many winemakers, it seems that this ability to hold one's nerve and not rush to intervene with additives or mechanical processes while the wine is being made is what marks out sheep from goats in terms of quality winemaking.

For organic winemakers the decision is simple: when in doubt, don't intervene. Wine, they'll tell you, should be a product of locality, weather conditions, soil and grape. It should be allowed to speak for itself and suffer as little human mucking-about as possible. So use the yeast God or the vine gave you, and leave it to do its work. As winemaker James Millton explains: 'It's easy to stand back if you have sensitivity, difficult if you are employing people who have been taught wine*making*. If the grapes are good it is a good experience to see what happens if you let them speak for themselves.'

PUTTING THE GRAPES TO WORK

It's vital to get the picked grapes into the winery as quickly as possible. The sun's heat acts fast, turning fresh, lively grapes to flabby, oxidised things in next to no time. Some conventional producers will use sulphur at this point to keep air and grape apart. Cannier producers will harvest when it's cooler.

So, assuming healthy grapes, what are the key things to watch for in the winery?

FERMENTATION

On arrival at the winery, grapes are crushed and destemmed prior to fermentation. For black grapes, the 'must' – the flesh, skins and juice – is pumped into a fermentation vat. White wine is fermented without the skins so the grapes are pressed before fermentation. The first key task is then to keep a watchful eye on the temperature the grapes ferment at. Just as cool washes are supposed to stop colours fading, so cool fermentation keeps the freshness of flavour in, and stops the wine 'cooking'. Chilling the fermentation vat – by running cold water down its outside, say – is what makes it possible to produce decent wine in hotter climates. It also, however, tends to produce white wines that don't taste of very much. They tend to be crisp, fresh, dry, neutral (CFDN) – and cheap, which is why so many of my tasting notes for wines around the £3 mark consist simply of CFDN. (And indeed too many wines at over £4 get this tasting note too, and at this level we really do deserve something better.) Keeping temperatures low also helps avoid heavy use of sulphur because wines are more stable at lower temperatures.

Second, there's the question of the means of fermentation. Grapes come pre-equipped to be turned into wine; that bloom on the grape skin contains millions of wild yeast cells, poised to do their duty as soon as conditions allow. But should the winemaker allow it? Many winemakers today prefer to use cultured yeast. They say they can control the process more scientifically that way, using yeasts designed to perform under controlled conditions. (And of course genetically engineered yeasts can carry this process a stage further, offering undreamed-of control – if we let it happen.) In some parts of the world the vineyard air is full of naturally occurring yeasts that have worked with the vines for a century or more. But more and more frequently this yeast history is simply ignored. No wonder wines are beginning to taste alike.

SULPHUR

The one chemical sanctioned by just about everybody in the wine business, organic or otherwise, is sulphur, a chemical used to preserve wine since antiquity. Some conventional producers use it with abandon in both vineyard and winery. In the vineyard the vines themselves need it as a trace element; but it has been liberally sprayed to prevent mildew for over a century in parts of France, with the result that the soil there is now too acidic.

Most winemakers use sulphur in its dioxide form, SO_2. This is made when naturally occurring mined sulphur is heated into a liquid. Because it reacts so readily with oxygen it will stop wine oxidising (i.e. it gets to the air before the wine can be damaged by it). It protects the wine's character by inhibiting bacteria and wild yeast, and encourages quick, clean fermentation. It prevents the juice oxidising, or browning, on contact with air, just like a peeled apple turns brown if you leave it out too long.

In grape juice or wine the sulphur dioxide reacts with water molecules to form sulphites. The Romans knew all this, and so did the Egyptians. Sulphites are also a natural by-product of fermentation, up to around 20 parts per million. We even produce sulphites in our own bodies.

So far, so good. This is a natural part of winemaking that has been harnessed for centuries, and even mimics our own internal production. What could be wrong with that?

One problem is the smell – the sometimes overpowering smell of a burning match – that catches you at the back of the throat when you inhale a first noseful from the glass. While most of us can't detect it below 200 milligrams per litre (mg/l), the most sensitive among us will pick it up at a fraction of that. Soil Association regulations for organic certification in the UK permit maximum total SO_2 levels of 90 mg/l in dry reds and 100 mg/l in dry whites. This should be well below the threshold for most of us, and organic producers – indeed, most producers of quality wines – are at pains to keep sulphur levels to a bare minimum. This compares with maximum levels imposed by the EU on non-organic wine of 160 mg/l on dry reds and 210 mg/l on dry whites.

An over-heavy hand with the sulphur is often caused by fear – fear that the wine won't remain stable, causing problems in later life. No one relishes the prospect of having to give refunds on faulty bottles. Sometimes, too, sulphur is used to draw a veil over winemaking mistakes. Almost nobody produces wine without sulphur. You're likely to have huge problems keeping the wine stable and preventing bacterial activity without it. Some brave souls attempt it. Others won't think of working without it. For Fetzer Bonterra winemaker Bob Blue, sulphur is 'the magic bullet that allows us to make complex, aged wines. Organic apple juice may be sulphate-free, but it won't keep like wine. You wouldn't get apple juice that's three years old.'

A test for sulphur

If you're worried that your wine may contain a lot of sulphur, and you can't smell it (because it's only at very high levels of sulphur that you get that hit at the back of the nose) here's a trick you can use to test for it. Add a little bottled still water to a sample of the wine. This will drive off more sulphur, and over the course of a few minutes' gentle sniffing you'll get a surge of the stuff. This will then be followed by a wine that smells more fruity, because too much sulphur in the wine inhibits the fruit aromas. And this is where it's pertinent to ask why wine labels don't tell us what additives the bottle contains – and why, astonishingly, it's actually illegal to declare what is in the wine. Those of us wanting to avoid overdosing on sulphur would find this kind of information very useful indeed.

Maybe one of the reasons organic wine had such a bad reputation is the evangelism with which organic wineries in the 1970s and 1980s refused to sully their wines with sulphur. As a result their wines were wildly inconsistent, doing mad, unstable things in the bottle, reeking of old socks or worse. And all subsequent organic endeavours have been tarred with the same brush, leaving the new generation of really rather good winemakers having to prove themselves over and over again.

All the organic wine specialists should be able to point you towards wines with low or even no sulphur. Organic specialists such as Vinceremos and Vintage Roots (see Chapter 8) do carry a few sulphur-free wines. They will give you advice on which wines to select for no or minute levels of sulphur to experiment with. Just remember that there can be variations in the quality of what's in the bottle, so don't open such a bottle for that special occasion without having something else in reserve. Just in case. Many of us, while not actually allergic to sulphur, do have very low tolerance levels, and experimenting with these wines might just give you a new lease of wine enjoyment.

Bear in mind, however, that to stabilise a wine without sulphur you might have to resort to pasteurisation. In wine, this means rapid heating to 85°C (185°F), or for 'flash pasteurisation' to 95°C (203°F) – the equivalent of a boil wash. The wine is held at that temperature for a few seconds, then is cooled equally quickly.

No getting away from it: this is a brutal thing to do to a wine, and certainly should never be used on any wine that has the potential for ageing. After all, winemakers do all they can to keep fermentation temperatures down to say 20°C (68°F) for whites and 30°C (86°F) for reds – so what kind of treatment is this for a wine?

Bergerac winemaker Richard Doughty gave this response to the pasteurisation of wine: 'Pasteurisation could be interesting for sweet wines but in reality it changes the flavour by cooking the residual sugar. Eliminating the live yeast with heat would be nicer than big sulphur doses but caramelised wine is not much good either. Pasteur himself never envisaged pasteurising wine; he considered wine the only really healthy drink, free of dangerous bacteria killed by the alcoholic fermentation – unlike milk, water and even beer, which if made with dirty water is unhealthy.'

MALOLACTIC FERMENTATION

This is nothing to do with the initial, alcoholic fermentation; it's another fermentation which transforms appley, sharp malic acid into the softer lactic acid, reducing the wine's acidity. So it can be a very Good Thing for wines, especially reds, made in cooler climates. Many producers will induce the malolactic to smooth out the wine's rough edges – or simply to prevent the danger of the malo occurring naturally after the wine has been bottled, which will have unpredictable results. In pre-technology times this fermentation used to occur spontaneously as the winery warmed up again the following spring, to cries of alarm and despondency all round. Only since the middle of this century has the process been properly understood and mastered.

Malolactic fermentation tends to be used most with red wines meant for ageing, and certain whites. It's not wanted in wines designed to be drunk young, or indeed in most white wines, and the way to avoid it happening is, yes, sulphur again; or pasteurisation, filtration and sterile bottling.

MAKING THE WINE LOOK GOOD

We like our wine bright and clear, don't we? We think any form of cloudiness is a fault. No nasty bits of sediment lurking at the bottom of the bottle waiting to be stirred up by shaky handling, thank you very much. Because we as consumers set such store on wine being clear, winemakers have gone to great lengths to oblige us. In their desire to please they can go too far, with the result that the baby is thrown out with the bathwater, and wine becomes brilliantly clear but also heartless – its soul sucked out by the brutal processes of fining and filtering.

There's an upside to this process, of course. It removes any bits that might be troublesome later on in causing the wine to re-ferment, or do all kinds of unpleasant things that stray bacteria lurking behind might encourage it to do.

FINING

Fining, in a nutshell, is for the impatient. Fining is the process of adding something to the wine that the suspended particles will cling to. When the fining agent precipitates out, caramba! Your wine is clear. Now there's a very good chance that the wine, left to itself, would fall bright anyway, but time is money, and let's get the wine out of the winery and on to the shelves as quickly as possible. And get paid.

Fining agents nowadays are designed with specific purposes in mind. If the wine has hard, bitter tannins in it, for instance, the fining agent can be used to remove these so that the wine acquires instant smoothness and palatability. Tannin preserves wine and without tannin it won't keep, but so what? The cost savings to the producer are enormous, and once it's out of the cellar he's not going to worry how much longer it'll last.

What's really used to fine wine?
This is where problems for vegetarians and vegans creep in. Wine is a vegetable product, right? No animal input? Wrong. There very often is. Fining agents that might trouble vegetarians include dried ox blood (rarely used now, fortunately), or isinglass, made from fish bladders. Vegans might be alarmed at the use of egg whites or casein, a milk protein. And after the mad cow scare, who wants to drink a wine fined with gelatine – made from cattle bones?

Safest from veggie and vegan points of view might be bentonite, a clay derived from aluminium. US research assures us that no traces of the bentonite remain when the wine has fallen bright. So that's all right then. Except that a heavy hand when dosing the wine can result in too many of the compounds that actually give the wine its flavour and character being removed.

The protein fining agents, the egg whites and fish bladders, do sometimes leave traces. Which is why, where I have the information, I've included a note in the buying guide to tell you which wines are suitable for vegetarians and vegans. Though in truth I believe it's more about squeamishness at the thought of what might have passed through the wine, than the danger of actually ingesting any traces of it.

These fining agents may appear unsettling, but it could be worse. Potassium ferrocyanide was once used as a fining agent, in very old wineries where the old copper or iron pipes hadn't been replaced by the now ubiquitous stainless steel. Wine acids would attack these old pipes, and the copper or tin from the pipes would cause a haze which the potassium ferrocyanide would remove in a process known as blue fining. The process is now widely outlawed because of fears that prussic acid – hydrogen cyanide! – could be formed in the process and remain in the wine.

Richard Doughty is clear that both fining and filtering are not a good idea. 'To make a deposit-free wine two months after harvest you have to massacre it. Suppose some nitwit has let his juice become enriched in iron. In non-organic rules you can fine with ferrocyanide and carefully filter out the crystals with your cyanide

---

Trace elements

Here's another copper-piping story, about beer this time, from Simon Loftus of Adnams wine merchants (see Chapter 8), who also make rather fine beers. Adnams were having trouble with a beer fermentation – a yeast infection, apparently, which is never welcome – and, even after overcoming the infection, the fermentation wasn't proceeding too well. Finally an old hand piped up: 'What about zinc?' Traces of zinc would have been naturally present in the brew in the days of copper pipes, but now they'd converted to stainless steel there could be no incidental take-up of this unregarded trace element. So they added one part per million of zinc – and the fermentation went through the roof. They finally settled on one quarter part per million.

This demonstrates how vital trace elements are, even in such minute, homeopathic quantities. And, as Simon concluded, if that tiny trace of zinc can make all the difference to the success of his fermentation, how can we trust government reassurances about the safety of pesticide residues in our food?

---

in them. The wine will be stable and "non-poisonous" but for me it's better to keep your juice and wine away from rusty iron.'

FILTERING

Filtering is, basically, the coffee filter writ large. Suspended particles are strained out of the wine through some sort of sieve or filter. This is a process for winemakers prepared to throw money at large pieces of stainless steel equipment rather than wait and trust that the wine will settle down by itself. It will eventually lower production costs by allowing you to sell the wine rather than have it hanging around the cellar cluttering up the place, so the decision depends a lot on the winemaker's philosophy.

It is done either with a sheet filter of some thick material such as cellulose powder or perlite, or a membrane filter – a thin film of plastic perforated with holes tinier than the particles to be trapped. The winemakers let the bits (lees) settle out of the wine and fall to the bottom of the vat. Then, to remove the lees, they siphon the wine off the lees. This process is called racking. Then there may be several filtrations, starting with a relatively coarse one and progressing to ever finer perforations, right down to a final filter which contains holes smaller even than the potentially destabilising yeasts and bacteria. The idea of this is to render the wine sterile. Sterile means risk-free. No likelihood of something nasty subsequently happening in the bottle.

For red wines, maturing in barrels helps it become stable and means filtration is less necessary. I firmly believe that filtration robs a decent wine of character and flavour, and I would like to see us consumers recognise that a sediment thrown in the bottle is a good, not a bad, sign. (White crystals in a bottle of white wine are another good sign, by the way. These are tartrates: more of them later.) Some specialist merchants have taken it upon themselves to educate us about unfiltered wines. Some, like Adnams' Simon Loftus, have gone a stage further, encouraging the producers he imports from to stop filtering the heart out of their wines.

Loftus's encouragement comes in the form of a guarantee to his producers: he will not return any bottle to them which has been rejected by a consumer on the grounds that it has bits in; that it hasn't been filtered. This, you see, is one of the main fears producers who filter have about stopping the practice. They believe their wines will be rejected by consumers and cost them money to replace. Loftus's guarantee means they can experiment and, for many of these producers, stopping filtering is the first step to going organic.

Richard Doughty sums it up: 'I'm a great partisan of leaving wine the time to fall bright. Or even wait a long time, and if it's not perfectly deposit-free well, never mind. Bottle it, sell it and explain to the people who drink it that the deposit is natural and more a sign of healthy, tasty wine than a problem or fault in the wine.'

TARTRATES

These are harmless crystals that precipitate out of wine during fermentation and ageing. They are another good sign, again indicating a wine that hasn't been mucked about with. Many producers, fearing adverse customer reaction (to the uninitiated, the crystals do look alarmingly like shards of glass), prefer to do unspeakable things to the wine to force the crystals to precipitate out rather than waiting until the crystals feel like it. This will probably be some time after bottling when the producer has finally relinquished control over the wine. And giving up control, sitting back and letting nature take its course, is the thing many winemakers find it hardest to do.

So what they do to 'stabilise' the wine is chill it well below freezing for a period of time. This forces the tartrates out. Then they filter the precipitated crystals out of the wine. An even faster technique involves chilling, adding potassium acid tartrate to the wine round which the tartrates will crystallise, and then immediately filtering.

Fining and filtering are the two surest ways to strip a wine of life and character. Some certified organic producers do both. Some conventional producers do neither. So if you're looking for a mark of quality winemaking that has nothing to do with pesticide application but everything to do with respect for your product, look for sediment in the bottom of the bottle. This is the crucial way to know that a wine hasn't been mucked about with. In so many cases, those fears are what prompt producers to fine and filter – fear that the wine won't be stable; fear that consumers won't accept a wine with 'bits' in.

But from our side as consumers, distrust of bits is mostly ignorance – if we don't know what the sediment signifies, of course we're going to think it's a fault. But if we know how to value it, we can accord wines made this way the status they deserve. And, of course, the more we demand unfiltered wines the more we'll get them – better for us, better for the wine.

OTHER WAYS OF BEATING NATURE IN THE WINERY

Acidity is one of the elements that give a wine character: one of the keys to good winemaking is to balance the sugar and the acids in the wine. Acidity too low means the wine tastes dull and flabby; too high, and you'll think you're drinking lemon juice – tart, mouth-puckering. You usually detect acidity in a wine via a pricking sensation on either side of the tongue.

Acidity and sugar are both present inside the ripening grape. In an under-ripe grape, acids predominate; as the sun reaches the grape and ripens it, sugars grow and acidity decreases. Thus the key to correct harvesting is to pick at the moment of perfect balance (which is why, of course, harvesting machines are so popular – picking at the optimum moment is much easier).

Picking too late means there will be less acidity, and in hot countries, like Australia, it's common to have to correct the balance with chemicals such as tartaric or citric acid.

Cool countries, like Germany, prize sugar content over everything else because the sun can't be relied upon. So their entire quality ladder is predicated on ever higher sugar levels in the wine. If there isn't enough sun, winemakers have two options: de-acidify, or bung in a few kilos of sugar to raise the alcohol content a degree or two. This is called chaptalisation, after Monsieur Chaptal who first got rid of his surplus sugar this way. The sun in a bag, some call it. Organic producers in Germany are forbidden to do this, and must rely on what nature gives them each year. This leads, you might say, to a more honest expression of what those vines can offer. Yes indeed.

After all, is this really what we want done in our name? Does 'the consumer' truly want wines that have been fined, filtered, centrifuged (like being put through a spin dryer), pasteurised, chaptalised, acidified? Maybe we *can* hold out for more naturally made wines. Our confidence in organic products, and our willingness to accept – no, prize – wines with bits in the bottle, will encourage better winemaking all over the world. We'll all benefit if producers start listening to the wine.

5
GENETIC MANIPULATION AND MODIFICATION:
HOW IT AFFECTS VINES

WINEMAKING HAS COME a long way since the days when the vine was a forest plant clinging in a tight tangle to trees, competing with other plants for light and nutrients, its grapes fermenting where they fell. Fermentation is a natural process which can occur without any human intervention, at a basic 'grape meets yeast' level. And because grape juice ferments quickly, the making of wine doesn't even imply agriculture: nomadic tribes can make wine of some sort within 24 hours. Winemaking in one form or another is probably as old as humanity.

All grapes will ferment, but the species *Vitis vinifera* does it best – it gives the largest and sweetest berries. This species probably originated south of the Black Sea around Georgia and Armenia (close to Mount Ararat, where Noah is supposed to have planted the first vines in the wake of the Flood). Greeks, Carthaginians and Romans were all expert in the art of winemaking, developing most of the pruning and training practices we fondly think of as modern.

While collecting grapes growing wild and making wine from them is a casual, opportunist activity, anyone settling down to farm grapes and produce wine in decent quantities will seek out the highest-yielding vines producing the largest, sweetest berries. *Vitis vinifera* will quickly revert to its wild form if left untended, producing smaller, more acidic berries. So farmers began to select from what they grew, taking cuttings and grafting, haphazardly at first, then systematically.

Working with vines' genetic material has developed in two stages:

firstly manipulation, which involves selecting certain vines and reproducing from their genetic material. This is called cloning. The second stage is genetic modification, which involves inserting genes from alien species – petunias, say, or broccoli, or even salmon – into the plant.

GENETIC MANIPULATION: SEND IN THE CLONES

Forget Dolly the sheep. Cloned vines have been a reality in the world's vineyards for decades. Grape growers have long noticed that individual vines growing cheek-by-jowl in the vineyard may have markedly different properties: ripening earlier or later, yielding more or less fruit, showing different levels of disease resistance or quality of flavour. Producers learned to identify superior vines, chosen for high yield, say, or good ripening. They took cuttings, propagated them and, after maybe 15 years of trials, ending up with row upon row of identical siblings from the 'mother vine'.

This was first achieved in Germany in 1926, and Germany remains the country that practises cloning most extensively. They have even made further selections from their original cloned vineyards, ending up with 'sons of clones'. New Zealand took this to its ultimate conclusion. There, every Sauvignon Blanc vine planted before the early 1990s could be traced to a single clone imported from the US. And we wonder why wines are beginning to taste the same ...

But there are problems with cloning other than homogeneity. It's good to improve wine quality, of course it is. And one thing clonal selection can do is select out incidence of virus disease, which is also extremely useful.

But what is this process of selection? Once there were large populations of plants in any field or vineyard. Plant breeders have worked for a long time to refine and reduce these to give greater yields and thus increase income. The downside of reducing biodiversity in this way, of course, is what happens when disaster strikes. As of course it will.

Take the Irish potato famine, for instance. A new disease struck this staple food, and nearly two million Irish people died. Or take the new strain of blight that attacked American corn in 1970, destroyed 50 per cent of the crop and bankrupted many farmers.

The effect of these disasters was intensified by the fact that in Ireland just two potato varieties were planted, both of which succumbed. And in the case of the corn, in common with most modern commercial crops, fewer than four varieties dominated the planting. Fewer varieties means more risk of crop wipe-out.

What do plant breeders do in the face of disease? Find plants with natural immunity to that disease from which to breed new, resistant varieties. They find these in remote rural areas, often in the developing world – the places where the plants originally came from. But guess what? Even the most remote places on the planet have now been reached by enterprising seed salespeople, and now these supposedly backward peasant communities grow the new varieties instead – so most of the old varieties have disappeared. As the Henry Doubleday Research Association, home of much innovative organic research, points out: 'The prospects for plant breeders, and for the security of the world's food supply, are worrying indeed.'

The idea of making a small population from a big population, and then making a big population again, worries many people. For Loire winemaker Nicolas Joly, passionate proponent of biodynamics, clonal selection is anathema. 'It's like going into a school and saying we only want the ten best pupils. But every one is useful, even the last one. It reminds me of Hitler.'

Surely that's the key here – a wide population mix brings character and diversity. Some Bordeaux châteaux, recognising this, practise clonal selection within the confines of their vineyard, emphasising the connection between the vines and their particular patch of soil. But for most producers, clones will be brought from hundreds of miles away. They'll be good-quality, high-yielding, disease-resistant vines – but will they have any individuality? Will they be sufficiently diverse to create a unique wine, or will the wines they make just taste like part of a great international wine lake? What to plant is one of the most important choices an organic grower must make.

An interesting thing about vine behaviour is the relatively high incidence of spontaneous mutation. Vines will sometimes mutate for no apparent reason, i.e. the genetic material just ups and changes during cell division. Pinot Noir is a particular culprit. Mutated vines will sometimes create multiple sets of chromosomes, producing giant plants and berries. Or they'll have albino leaves or berries. The point is that vines don't always behave in predictable ways. And, as we'll see as we move on to genetic modification, science places a great deal of reliance on the idea that it can alter one part of the vine without that affecting any other part. Ha!

Genetic modification: Frankenstein Frascati

If clonal selection can worry you, genetic modification will give you nightmares. Mutations are just the start.

Terms first. All these words mean the same thing: genetic modification, genetically engineered, transgenic, recombinant DNA, gene tinkering, Frankenstein foods, and (I like this one!) pharming.

They all refer to the splicing of genes from one organism to another, unrelated, organism, to produce in combination a trait that would be very unlikely to occur naturally. The technology is currently more advanced in agriculture than it is in viticulture because the financial return in agriculture is faster. It's also harder to engineer genetic modifications in woody plants such as vines. But these difficulties have been overcome and vinous genetic modification is surging forward. That's why it's instructive to look at what's happening in agriculture, because it points the way to a possible future for vines too – if we let that happen.

At the moment, around two-thirds of all commercial agricultural applications involve creating herbicide tolerance in field crops. An example of this is Roundup-Ready seed. Roundup is a glyphosate herbicide produced by Monsanto who have created genetically modified (GM) seeds such as cotton and soya that show resistance to Roundup, and Roundup only.

Before genetic modification you could only spray Roundup before planting as it would have killed every living thing in sight indiscriminately (and, of course, it still does – a poison is a poison). But now you plant the GM seeds, and when the weeds come you can spray with Roundup again. This would normally kill both weeds *and* crops, but the GM seeds are resistant and survive. Spray with a competitor's herbicide, of course, and you lose everything. And if you spray repeatedly you can be sure that weeds will increase their resistance to the specific herbicide you're using. So you'll need to squirt on even more Roundup simply to maintain the same level of weed control.

In 1987, a tolerance level of six parts per million (ppm) was set for glyphosate residues in foodstuffs. This was increased to 20 ppm just as the first Roundup-Ready crops went on stream in the 1990s. Thus you can blame genetic engineering for an increase in poison residues in our food.

THE TERMINATOR GENE

Not content with tying you in for one season, the GM companies want to tie you in forever. That's where the Terminator gene comes in. Terminator technology introduces a gene (three, actually) into the plant which forces it to produce a toxin which kills its own seed. It won't be back.

Hang on a minute. Don't these companies try to sell themselves to us by claiming that this new technology will solve worldwide hunger? How does it feed the world if 1.4 billion farmers in third-world countries can no longer do what they've done for centuries and save their seed to sow next year? Especially if pollen from Terminator plants can travel out of the Terminated fields – pollen can travel up to 8 km (5 miles) if there are lots of bees to carry it. This means it can pollinate plants in nearby fields and render them sterile. No seed to sow next year. That'll go a long way to solve starvation, won't it?

Terminator 2

This is a sophisticated refinement of Terminator technology. Here the companies have brought back the Terminator as a 'Lazarus gene', able to wake seed from the dead. The seed is still programmed to die at the end of the growing season, but can be revived by buying the company's chemicals to spray the following spring. So much easier for the GM companies than having to distribute new seed each year.

I take heart, in all of this nightmare profiteering, from the fact that at the end of the movie *Terminator 2*, the Terminator destroys himself to save mankind.

And what about genetic pollution? Where an organic farmer's crops are cross-fertilised by wind-borne GM pollen? As an organic farmer, what recourse would you have against such biological contamination of your land? The company that created Terminator is to be bought by Monsanto for a reported 1.9 *billion* dollars. That's what Terminator technology is worth.

THE 'ORGANIC' PESTICIDE: BT

Another pesticide in wide use – even by organic farmers – is Bt, based not on a chemical but on a bug, *Bacillus thuringiensis*. This naturally occurring bacterium is toxic to caterpillars (and butterflies and beetles, unfortunately) but finds favour in certain organic circles because it occurs naturally in the soil and is inert, minding its own business and doing no damage until ingested by an unsuspecting caterpillar, when it does a great deal of damage to its insides. Registered since 1961, it was hailed as the perfect pesticide because it specifically targeted certain pests without having a detrimental effect on mammals, birds or (most) non-target insect species and micro-organisms.

Not any more. The GM industry has appropriated 'the single most important pesticide ever discovered' for its own ends. Bt resistance has been noted since 1981, and organic producers are anxious to minimise all potential for growing Bt resistance. So what does the GM industry do? Engineer Bt into the permanent genetic code of plants. The US is already growing 60 million acres of Bt-engineered corn.

This will soon lead to Bt resistance in major pests. Wild plants will probably acquire Bt genes through cross-pollination. In addition, the Bt produced by transgenic plants differs from the original bacterium and accumulates in the soil. So in February 1999, IFOAM (the International Federation of Organic Agriculture Movements), Greenpeace and 70 others are suing the US Environmental Protection Agency for the wanton destruction of the world's most important biological pesticide.

The problem all along in conventional agriculture and viticulture has been an inability to see that biological systems are ecological, or holistic – that is, things that happen in the vineyard or field are a result of many interacting factors, not simply Cause A leading to Effect B. Chemical, and now transgenic, agriculture sees a problem and finds a solution, forgetting that the solution is likely to bring several more problems in its wake. Fix one problem and create several more.

Genetic modifications made to vines

Apart from this threat to all organic farmers, what's happening specifically in the field of viticulture? Vines haven't been subject to the same intensive research and engineering, probably because, as perennials, there isn't such a big opportunity to make a quick billion.

Yeasts have been coming under scrutiny from the GM industry, and Stanford University in the US has assembled a database with as many ideas as the imagination can contemplate, endless refinements and perversions of the winemaking process. You could theoretically create a yeast for any fermentation and flavour – so who needs a specific site?

Stellenbosch University, South Africa, is playing with a GM yeast for malolactic fermentation. Champagne house Moët et Chandon has genetically modified Chardonnay vines to resist fanleaf virus and is close to being able to use them commercially. Canada is field-testing transgenic vines that are more resistant to cold. Paul Bosc, head of the Ontario winery where the trials are being carried out, said: 'These vines have been given a winter jacket.' (All together now: aaaah.) 'There will be no change in the flavour, colour or texture of the grape and it will still produce the finest Cabernet Franc.'

One question. How does he know?

The one thing we know about vines is their ability to mutate almost at will. How can he, or anyone, know in advance what the results of tinkering with the genetic make-up of vines will be?

In an Australian article, under the breathless headline 'Transgenic vines could save $100 million a year', molecular biologist Dr Nigel Scott describes Australia's first transgenic vine, a project backed by over five million Australian dollars. He's focusing on disease resistance and reducing labour costs, using an American hybrid rootstock called Seyval which is resistant to powdery mildew (hybrids are banned in Europe, but let that pass).

Dr Scott has also isolated the gene that affects the grape's colour and is looking at changing the alcohol or sugar levels that interact with the genes controlling flavour. He's already done it with tomatoes: increasing levels of certain alcohols in tomatoes has apparently achieved 'more desirable smells, indicating an improved flavour'.

Forgive me, but I find the idea of playing God in this way completely repellent. Tomatoes are perfectly capable of producing excellent smell and taste all by themselves, thank you very much. All you have to do is choose decent varieties – flavour, not uniformity of shape – and grow them as nature intended.

You know, it's not much of a leap of imagination from the place this scientist is already at to the nightmare scenario put to me by Dr Tony Jordan of Wirra Wirra winery in South Australia. He explained that once you can isolate flavour compounds you can insert the desirable flavours of, say, New Zealand Sauvignon Blanc into Sauvignon Blanc grown in the Barossa Valley in South Australia, where crops perform more reliably in the better climate. 'You could introduce triggers into the Sauvignon Blanc that would trigger accumulations of the New Zealand flavour compound.'

Riesling's another good example. 'It's a wonderful grape when grown in cool climates, but at hotter temperatures the elegant aromas don't come out so well – the flavour compounds get locked up in the juice. You can buy enzymes which unlock these aromas, which you add to the wine. Why not genetically alter the yeast so that the yeast produces the same enzyme?'

Well, why not take all this a stage further. If you can isolate the flavour compound which makes a grape perform well in, say, the top châteaux of Bordeaux, you can genetically modify Cabernet vines and plant them somewhere hot and cheap like Algeria and produce wines like Château Lafite for £3.49. Grape variety and location could become totally irrelevant – all you'd have to do is insert a combination of genes to produce the desired traits in whatever vine you happened to be planting. Bye-bye terroir, individuality, character.

And maybe, eventually, bye-bye vine. Remember what happened in Ireland and the US when too little biodiversity led to the destruction of harvests. Any pest or disease could mutate and wipe out the lot. It could even be man-made – the brewing industry has already discovered how to insert grape traits into barley crops and is now producing a wine-flavoured brew – at half the cost again of winemaking from GM grapes.

We've opened Pandora's box, and whatever happens the lid will never be closed again. All we can now do is to speak out and fight back wherever practicable. Because all is not lost. In March 1999 the Washington appeal court took up the legal testing of the idea that major food crops can be patented – so all those lovely lucrative GM patents may be under threat from Congress. Greenpeace and Friends of the Earth continue to campaign on these issues.

In many ways the tide already seems to be turning – all over the world. Japan's major breweries have rejected GM ingredients. Deutsche Bank, the world's largest bank, has advised its investors to sell shares in companies developing GM crops because of 'growing negative sentiment'. In a 1999 report they observed that 'increasingly, GM organisms are in our opinion becoming a liability to farmers'. US grain merchants are now paying a premium of around 10 per cent for export-bound soya and corn that hasn't been genetically modified.

What turned the tide? Consumer pressure. And if we did it once, we can do it again. If we continue to exert pressure for more food and wine to be produced organically you can be sure the market will respond. The acreage of vineyards in France under conversion to organic is exploding (see pages 89–91). The amount of land farmed organically in the UK rose by an amazing 500 per cent between April 1998 and April 1999. However, that's still less than 3 per cent of agricultural land. There's a way to go yet. The single most important thing we can all do is vote with our wallets and buy organic.

6
BIODYNAMICS:
HEALING THE VINEYARD

PICTURE THE SCENE: a biting January day in the Loire valley in northern France, sun shining but wind howling and bitterly cold. I'm coming to the end of my first wine research trip to France. This is the last estate visit and part of my brain is already wondering what time we'll have to leave to catch the ferry home. But, though I didn't realise it at the time, I'd stumbled on to something that would have a profound impact on me. This was a biodynamic wine estate, and at the end of interviewing the winemaker I walked out into the vineyard. In January, of course, the vines are dormant. No growth, just rows of neatly pruned bare woody plants, sleeping.

Yet, standing alone among the bare vines, I had an overwhelming sense that the vineyard was *alive*. It positively hummed, vibrated with life. It was an extraordinary sensation, quite unlike anything I had experienced in a vineyard – or indeed on any patch of land – before. How could it possibly be full of life in January? Yet the evidence assailing all my senses was undeniable. I realised that there had to be something different about biodynamics, and from that moment I wanted to know more.

As I began to write books on French wine tourism, I would prick up my ears whenever someone suggested visiting a biodynamic estate. I had a long discussion on the subject with Michel Chapoutier in the Rhône, and he lent me a copy of the seminal text on the subject, *Agriculture*, by Austrian scientist and seer Rudolf Steiner.

This book was nearly my undoing. *Agriculture* is not light bedtime reading. I just couldn't get my brain round it and it nearly put me off altogether. I now know that this text is not recommended for the beginner (too right) but it does contain the basic principles that biodynamic grape growers follow today.

RUDOLF STEINER: CREATOR OF BIODYNAMICS

Steiner was born in rural Austria in 1861, at a time when the new world of science and technical understanding was colliding with ancient peasant wisdom. What Steiner did was to synthesise these two apparently warring worlds. He studied modern science and philosophy and then integrated this learning with his own clairvoyant spirituality. Out of this he developed a 'spiritual science' he called anthroposophy, meaning the inherent wisdom of humanity. Many people find in this vision of human potential much hope for the regeneration and renewal of the planet, and his work is now studied and implemented all over the world.

Steiner's influence is visible today in such areas as education (Waldorf schools), adult education, medicine, eurythmy (healing movement and gesture) and the Camphill communities, which support adults with learning difficulties.

The impetus for biodynamic agriculture came from a group of farmers active in anthroposophy who were deeply concerned about the decline in seed and soil fertility. In 1924, the year before he died, Steiner delivered a series of eight lectures to them called 'Towards a spiritual renewal in agriculture', and it's these lectures that are published today as *Agriculture*.

HOW BIODYNAMICS DIFFERS FROM ORGANICS

Organic grape growing is (as I do hope I've demonstrated) a very Good Thing. It takes the laboratory out of the vineyard, ignoring chemicals and artifice in favour of working with nature. The organic grape grower observes what nature does and tries to follow it – combating insect pests with predator pests, companion planting and so on. Many growers express the wish to do as little damage as possible to their environment, so they can pass the vineyard on to their children in good condition. Walking lightly on the earth and all that.

Biodynamics takes a different jumping-off point, and moves one step beyond the organic stance of following nature's lead and working in harmony with it. In biodynamics, the belief is that all the chemical inputs and bad practice of conventional intensive viticulture have damaged the planet. The decline in soil and seed fertility was noticed 100 years ago and now we're witnessing a decline in human fertility too. This, the theory goes, needs to be counteracted. Don't simply let nature run its course, but instead support and intensify natural processes to heal vineyards damaged by decades of pollution. There are several ways biodynamics does this:

- detailed observation of what's going on in the vineyard, seeking to understand what's really happening
- using special herbal sprays on the land and on compost
- fighting pests with homeopathy
- enhancing life-force energy in the grapes
- working on the vines when the planetary constellations are most favourable
- working according to moon phase
- harnessing the four elements: earth, air, fire, water
- using human thought processes and consciousness

'Biodynamics' comes from two Greek words meaning life and energy and it involves working with all the energies that create and maintain life. In this system you want to harness all the forces around you – not just the sun, but the moon, stars and the earth itself (the whole cosmos, really). See all these as one constantly interacting whole and it becomes clear that there's more to draw on to get the best out of the grapes.

I'll admit that some aspects of biodynamism can sound a bit way out if you're new to it, but it's won some hard-headed converts at the very heart of the wine world – top winemakers like Anne-Claude Leflaive of Domaine Leflaive and Lalou Bize-Leroy of Domaine Leroy, both in Burgundy; Nicolas Joly of Savennières and Didier Dageneau of Pouilly-Fumé, both in the Loire; and Michel Chapoutier down in the Rhône.

FOCUSING ON LIFE-FORCES

Key to it all is life-force energy. That, perhaps more than anything, is what marks biodynamics out from organics. We're talking about spirit here, the energising force, consciousness, the thing that makes us who and what we are. It's the difference between being alive and being dead, basically. It's like that sad moment when relatives go to pay their last respects at the undertaker's, then come out saying: 'It wasn't Grandma – she's gone.' The body, the shell, is still there, but what animated it, made it who she was, has departed.

What's the difference between an apple eaten straight from the tree, and one that's been picked green, ripened in a gas house and irradiated to stop it rotting? The seeds of an irradiated apple can never germinate. You could say it's dead. Biodynamics puts a value on the *quality* of what we eat in terms of its life-force – it's not just matter to be consumed, not just a question of calories and carbs.

The other key thing is to focus on life not death. The more I talk to conventional grape growers the more obsessed they seem to be with killing off every last pest and weed and fungus that dares to invade their precious patch. Biodynamic and organic grape growers tend to take a more relaxed view of weeds and pests. As Bergerac winemaker Richard Doughty points out, a few insects pose no problem: 'I don't do anything to them and they don't do any significant damage to my vines. It amazes me to see winemakers spending lots of money on nasty poisons to eliminate bugs. When you start killing predators, the surviving bugs, now minus predators, will overfeed and you get problems. If you let nature get on with it, the absence of problems is quite stunning except for ICI shareholders.'

As they say in these circles, what you think, you grow. Focus on disease and what will you get? You'll get what you focus on, so you might as well focus on what you want rather than what you don't want. And in viticulture it's a good idea to focus on ripe, healthy fruit, not on your brave, lonely battle against pests and diseases.

Biodynamics is also interested in the opposite of gravity, woefully translated as 'levity' (mind you, I think a bit of levity around such a complicated subject is no bad thing). That's to say, gravity is what makes the apple fall off the tree; levity is the study of how it got up there in the first place. Funny how we trust science based on gravity and don't allow for exploration of a possible counterpart; gravity is the only scientific concept which doesn't have a polar opposite – positive and negative electricity, hot and cold, wet and dry, gravity and ...

CYCLES AND RHYTHMS

The whole of the growth cycle of grapes, and of everything else on the planet, is one of expansion and contraction. See the earth as a living organism in its own right and this begins to make sense. The astronauts, when they left the planet and looked back at it as an entity, felt this most strongly.

So imagine the earth breathes, has a circulation system, a pulse and a skin. Water provides the circulation system: rain to rivers to seas to mists. The movement of the seasons acts as a kind of pulse, expanding in spring and summer then contracting in autumn and winter. The earth's skin consists of soil and plants, spreading like scar tissue across barren landscapes – look how fast the side of a motorway cutting will green over, or your freshly hoed vine rows, or even the sides of a slag heap.

The earth itself is said in biodynamics to have a daily as well as an annual contraction/expansion cycle, so the first rhythm to observe is that of the day: as the earth breathes out in the morning and in again in the afternoon. Flower petals open and close in precise patterns according to this daily rhythm, so accurately that in the eighteenth century they planted flower clocks in gardens which told the time by the opening and closing of the petals. We have these daily (circadian) rhythms too, as any daysleeper who's struggled to overcome jet lag after crossing several time zones knows only too well. So, to work with this rhythm, biodynamic grape growers lift the young vine plants in the morning, and put them aside for planting out in the contracting period of the afternoon.

THE SUN

This star gives us all the warmth and light we need to grow. As it gets higher in the sky from midwinter to midsummer it draws the growth cycle of plants up with it. Then, as it starts to wane, we move to harvest and the earth itself draws in the life-force received from the sun in the summer. The sun is the biggest example there is of 'levity', the expansive force.

The angle of the sun's rays focus deep into the earth in the short December days. As the days lengthen the angle gradually rises until it arrives on the surface on March 21, when day and night are of equal length. From here it moves out into the air, along with the rapidly growing plants, reaching its highest point at the summer solstice. Then it sinks slowly back down, touching the surface again at the autumn equinox, and going back into the soil.

These four cardinal points of the year form feast days and celebrations all over the world. Pagan festivals occupied these slots in the UK until Christianity supplanted them. For example, 24 and 25 December are the first days when there's a perceptible increase in the length of day over night, which is when Christians celebrate the arrival of the Light of the World.

Easter Sunday always falls on the Sunday nearest the full moon after the spring equinox. This is the time when levity, the rising principle, is strongly in operation – plants defy gravity and rise out of the earth, mirroring, as Christians point out, the resurrection of Christ.

Each year, biodynamic experts issue planting calendars telling vineyard workers what to do when, because it's quite complicated. And each year, the calendar says do nothing at all to the vines on Good Friday and Easter Saturday. Some say that this is because Christ's suffering is so deeply imprinted into the earth. Others point to the adverse planetary arrangements on those two days. I just think it's really interesting that it should be so, year after year. And what about that old folk wisdom that says the best day to plant your potatoes is Easter Monday?

THE ZODIAC

Each year, as the earth moves round the sun, the sun appears in front of each of the 12 signs of the zodiac in turn, and the sun is said to have a different quality depending on which constellation it is in. The weak December sun has a very different quality to the fierce heat of midsummer, when it is in Gemini. As the sun begins its descent, passing through fiery Leo in August and the quieter Virgo in September, the sun touching our skin feels very different to the gathering warmth of the springtime sun.

If you think people are different according to their birth sign, ruled by the sun, then it isn't much of a stretch to think that the sun will itself radiate perceptibly different kinds of heat as it moves through each sign during the year.

THE MOON

If the sun controls light and heat on earth, the moon controls water – and not just the tides. Humans, grapes, all plants and animals, consist mostly of water. We spend the first nine months of our lives suspended in it, so it's not surprising it's familiar.

The moon moves through several simultaneous cycles each month, each taking more or less 28 days, all of them weaving around each other. The first and most obvious lunar cycle is the waxing and waning moon. The effects of the round full moon are already experienced by many. Police, bar staff, nursing staff in mental hospitals can all attest to differences in human behaviour when the moon is full (and of course we all know about were-wolves). More babies are born just before a full moon than afterwards. Repeated tests have shown it's best to sow seeds shortly before the full moon, in the second quarter of the lunar cycle, and weed or prune in the 'rest period' of the fourth quarter.

Another cycle is apogee/perigee, which looks at the distance the moon is from the earth. Closest to the earth (perigee) or furthest away (apogee) in each cycle makes a difference to what you do in the vine-yard. It's held to be best not to sow or plant on either of these.

Then, of course, you have the effect of each of the 12 constella-tions. While the sun passes through these only once every year, the moon passes through them all every 28 days; you get, in effect, a year in every month. This is very handy for biodynamic grape growers and winemakers. Certain processes are best carried out during certain moon phases, and each constellation has a different effect on what you do on the land.

THE FOUR ELEMENTS: EARTH, AIR, FIRE, WATER

Each of the 12 signs of the zodiac is assigned either to air (Gemini, Libra, Aquarius), water (Cancer, Scorpio, Pisces), fire (Aries, Leo, Sagittarius) or earth (Taurus, Virgo, Capricorn). This gives them a special connection with one of these four life-forces.

Plants, too, have connections with one or other of these life-forces. Biodynamics classifies plants according to which part of them is most developed and harvested: fruit, flower, leaf or root. Roots such as potatoes and carrots are, not unnaturally, connected with the earth element; flowers are connected with the air element; leafy vegetables and salads connect with the water element; and fruits – such as grapes – link up with the fire element.

Thus, as the moon passes through each of the 12 constellations each month, gardeners work on whichever type of plant the moon is currently governing. Twelves into 28 only go two and a bit, so you get just two or three days a month in each sign. Grape growers focus their attention on the times when the moon is in a 'fruit' phase.

And I haven't even mentioned the effects of eclipses (bad, do nothing outdoors) or the intersections of various planetary paths, called nodes (ditto). So it's really just as well that each year you can buy the annual planting calendar, *Gardening by the Stars and Constellations*, in which Maria Thun, a German farmer and researcher who has spent 40 years observing and testing these phenomena, has helpfully detailed what you can do when. Mind you, even then you have a lot of astronomical symbols to decipher before it makes sense. There's no doubt that this regime requires a level of dedication and commitment not required in more straight-forward organic viticulture.

Take picking, for instance. If you hire a team of grape pickers it can take them several weeks to move through the vineyards, depending on size of plot and team. Yet in the calendar you only have three picking days each cycle – fruit days during an ascending moon, to be precise. So what do you do? Hire a huge team and pick then, regardless of conditions? Watch the weather and pick when the climate is right, irrespective of calendar correctness? Or maybe bring out the picking machine and get it comfortably done in the lunar time frame, and worry about soil compaction from the machine's tyres later.

The planting calendar extends into the wine cellar too. You should bottle the wine on a fruit day in a descending moon, because, as Veronique Cochran of Château Falfas in Bordeaux explained, if you bottle during an ascending moon all the aromas that belong in the bottle will leave the wine and fill the cellar. If you bottle during a descending moon, she added, you keep the aromas where they belong. In the bottle.

The planting calendar can act as a wonderful motivator for the experts at procrastination among us. Noticing that you can only prune the vines in the next four hours or you'll have to wait until the following month (which will be too late) concentrates the mind wonderfully, and out come the secateurs. As James Millton in New Zealand points out, however: 'It does tend to intrude on the pleasures of life and although work is pleasure we still need to eat, drink, talk and be merry ...'

THE EARTH

Soil – tiny particles of minerals, humus, and micro-organisms. Conventional viticulture more or less ignores the soil. It sees it as something that cannot sustain life on its own, needing to be fed with large doses of water-soluble chemicals. The organic grape grower turns his or her back on synthetic chemistry, favouring a sustainable, ecologically sound approach, nurturing a healthy soil and sturdy, healthy vines. The biodynamic grape grower, while also emphasising ecological soundness, widens the scope to include all the influences that stream into the soil from the universe. They look to expand consciousness – not just in themselves, but in the soil and the vines they tend, looking into the deeper spirit of nature.

Biodynamics is possibly the finest antidote available to all those who despair that wines are starting to taste the same, worrying that they could come from anywhere (and, indeed, if genetic modification of vines goes the way it's currently heading, they *will* come from anywhere). Biodynamics focuses intently on the particular patch of soil that you call your own, and works to intensify its uniqueness. The French call this 'terroir', but unfortunately this is an elastic concept which they stretch to mean whatever they want it to mean. What I think 'terroir' should mean is uniqueness based on that site, a sense of 'somewhereness'. If you've ever had the happy occasion to wander round top vineyard sites, you do get a sense of why that land is special. Especially if it's cultivated biodynamically.

COMPOSTING

One way of nurturing the soil is through the use of manure and compost, and there are complex instructions for the preparation of compost heaps. Loire winemaker Nicolas Joly has taken the care of his soil to the final conclusion: wanting only to use biodynamic manure, he keeps his own herd of rare-breed cattle to provide it. He even grows corn for their straw – biodynamically, of course. This approaches the biodynamic ideal of the self-sustaining farm, which grows all its needs, recycles its own wastes, takes next to nothing from the environment and gives back as much as possible to the land and the surrounding community.

The use of cow manure is widespread in biodynamics, valued for the effect the cow's slow digestive process is held to have on the 'digestive process' of the earth, linking the vine roots to the soil. Vines, after all, grow where little else will; indeed, you don't want a rich soil or they'll overcrop like mad things. Joly has experimented with the effects of manure from different animals. Local people told him that if you are replanting vines, pig manure is best. He realised that pigs root for food underneath the soil, so this would give the vine roots a tendency to burrow deep. On the other hand, he said, you'll miss out on elegance in the wine: 'A pig is a pig after all, you can't change that.'

Enhancing nature: homeopathy

One of the main ways biodynamists support and heal a land stressed and weakened by the damage caused by intensive agriculture and industrial poisoning is by applying homeopathic sprays. The science of homeopathy is based on treating like with like to support nature's own processes. Its key principle, the Law of Similars, states that substances that produce specific symptoms in healthy individuals will cure the same symptoms in chronically ill patients. The homeopath's aim is to discover what natural substance, suitably 'energised', will restore balance in a particular individual.

To make a homeopathic preparation, make a solution of the herb in water or alcohol then progressively dilute it, shaking it each time to energise it. Keep on and on diluting and shaking, until at some massive dilution point the molecules of the original herb are not even present any more. All that's left is the energised, 'potentised' water.

Just water? So it can't work, can it? But it does. I've experienced it for myself, taking homeopathic belladonna which dramatically reduced a fever; and I've seen it work in others, too. (Incidentally, biodynamics and homeopathy meet in the natural remedies company Weleda, who grow 300 species of plants for their medicines biodynamically in Derbyshire.)

WATER AND THE BIODYNAMIC PREPARATIONS

Biodynamics calls for the use of several different sprays, to be used on the vines at different times and for different purposes. Several of the ingredients are also used in homeopathy – yarrow, camomile, nettle, dandelion, oak, horsetail, valerian. These sprays are used on the compost heap at various times to activate different elements in it.

Biodynamics prefers its preparations stirred not shaken, a distinction Pierce Brosnan would no doubt not appreciate, and calls the process 'dynamising'. To dynamise a biodynamic preparation, add a pinch of the herb to a bucket or barrel of water and stir it, vigorously and precisely, until a crater is created right to the bottom of your bucket. Then immediately reverse the direction of stir until a deep crater is formed again, whereupon you briskly reverse direction once more. For an hour. Keep reversing the direction quickly so the water seethes and tumbles, like water bursting forth from a dam or leaping down rocks.

Water worked upon in this way opens up a far greater surface area than a still surface; and that, they say, is what lets cosmic energy forces in, what dynamises it. It's a crucial part of the process, but it takes quite a lot of effort. Stirring on this scale doesn't appeal to everybody, and some grape growers set up Heath Robinson-like contraptions to do it for them. I've seen paddles suspended in half-barrels, beating away. Romantically, I fancy that your connection to your soil will be enhanced if you stir by hand, but let's be pragmatic: whatever works.

Then there are two sprays to be used directly on the vineyard. One is made with ground quartz and is sprayed on the vines to enhance light and warmth; the other is made from cow dung (and known as the horn dung preparation). First prepare the material to make the preparations from by burying them; all of them are buried over winter, except the quartz, which is buried throughout the summer. This preparation is known as 'horn quartz' or 'horn silica'. These last two are buried in cows' horns.

Then spray the preparations on the vines at times determined by the calendar for particular effects. The horn dung stimulates the connection to the earth, so it's the first one to use, at the start of the growing season. Horn quartz aids the light and warmth transmitting cosmic forces, so spray it, in the morning, directly on to the vine leaves or young grapes.

I don't think it's any coincidence that homeopathy grew out of the medieval science of alchemy, which sought to transmute base metal into gold. These preparations work an alchemy of their own, turning cow dung into humus and maybe even a sick and ailing vineyard into one teeming with life again.

The homeopathic principles of treating like with like are also invoked when it comes to dealing with insect pests. Simply collect a few specimens of the troublesome pests from the vineyard, then burn them and make a homeopathic solution with their ashes, or macerate them in water and make the solution from that. Then spray the solution on the vines, and the pests stay away. No, really, they do! It's as if a message flies round the bush telegraph: 'Look what happened to all our friends and relations. Better keep clear.' Or maybe it's the same principle that stops horses grazing near their own manure, though they'll quite happily forage near cow dung.

SCIENCE AND BIODYNAMICS

Biology, physics and chemistry, and indeed all areas of scientific research, are moving towards the idea that all science is simply part of the same thing. The basic building blocks of everything on the planet – you, me, that plant, that bottle – are just bits of energy. Know how that works, some say, and you'll know everything. So the most helpful viewpoint seems to be that everything depends on everything else. And that's a view shared by biodynamics.

Some aspects of biodynamics don't seem to have a rational explanation. But science can't explain everything either, and sometimes when new ideas and discoveries are first pronounced, those in the current scientific establishment ridicule the proponents (or excommunicate them. Or burn them at the stake as heretics). I think we've moved on somewhat since Copernican times, but anyone who wants to make spirituality a factor in science is still in for a very rough ride.

But how did science unfold? As a series of logically evolving discoveries, each built securely on the foundation of what went before? Far from it. Instead it seems to be a series of often wildly opposing points of view, the latest orthodoxy obliterating all that went before it. It's reasonable to assume that this process isn't over yet, and current orthodoxies could be swept away in the light of the next round of discoveries. That isn't to say that biodynamics has all the answers, or even that it's right; simply to note that just because it all sounds so unusual, that doesn't mean it can't produce excellent results.

BIODYNAMICS IN ACTION

Some people are unimpressed with biodynamic theory and have to be convinced by seeing the results in the vineyard. Veronique Cochran encountered some initial resistance from her workers at Château Falfas but reports that after two years they could see for themselves the difference in the quality of the soil.

Seeing biodynamics in action is also what convinced Thetford wine merchant Trevor Hughes of T&W Wines of its effectiveness – so much that he now devotes a two-page spread in his wine list to producers working biodynamically. 'For years I had a house just down the road from the Guillemots in Burgundy. I'd bought their wine for several years, and we became friends. They discussed their proposed changeover from organic to biodynamic, but I didn't become fully convinced that it works until I saw the changes in their soil and their vines. It all looked so alive, as if it had body and life and vitality. When they just farmed organically it never shone like that. When I compared their soil to that of their neighbours – especially those who had just sprayed – there was such a difference that I knew this must be the way to go.'

Trevor is quick to point out that farming biodynamically doesn't automatically produce good wine, citing the example of one prominent biodynamist who, he feels, produces terrible wines. But, as he says, 'The amount of effort biodynamic producers have to put in means you don't do it for effect or for publicity, you do it for pure love.'

It's remarkable how many of the all-time top wine estates in France are converting to biodynamic winemaking. More than anything else, this is what proves to me that the winds of change are blowing. These people are moving over to biodynamics because they know it works. And the proof of that is in the glass.

7
WHERE'S IT COMING FROM?
A COUNTRY-BY-COUNTRY GUIDE

ORGANIC WINE IS being made all over the world, even in the Canary Isles, but it's like anything else: standards vary enormously. I thought it would be interesting to look at it on a country-by-country basis – at least where information exists. It doesn't everywhere. Some countries, the smaller wine producing areas or the more backward, are more concerned with establishing themselves internationally than with monitoring what is going on from an organic point of view. Some simply don't think it sufficiently important to warrant gathering statistics about organic acreages and trends. And if conventional winemakers and farmers had to add to their prices the costs of undoing the environmental damage they do – such as removing the residues of pesticides they spray from our groundwater – organic prices would suddenly be lower than conventional ones. Then we'd know the true costs of production.

Jem Gardener of organic specialists Vinceremos points to difficulties in sourcing organic wines that will become more acute in the next 12 months. 'There is competition now from the Far East. Worldwide, there is rocketing demand, especially from Japan, not to mention North America and northern Europe. Some producers are selling to the highest bidder. There were low yields in 1997 and 1998, so producers were releasing vintages earlier than ever before because of demand.'

Cash flow is becoming more and more important to producers, so they're selling earlier and earlier, with the result that it becomes harder and harder to find red wines with any bottle age. Someone has to cellar the better wines to give them a chance to mature before drinking. Once upon a time this was done by the producers themselves, bottles slumbering romantically in cellars, or by wine merchants. But bottles are money. Liquidise the liquids. If you want a mature red organic wine, the chances are growing you'll have to do some of the cellaring yourself.

FRANCE

One of the few countries bothering to collect statistics for organic production, France currently has 5456 hectares (13,472 acres) of organic vines. Significantly for us, this figure increased by 27 per cent in 1998. An increase in organic production of over a quarter in just one year is phenomenal, and shows the level of commitment we're talking about. There's competition for every organic bottle, and the UK market has to fight for supply amid the burgeoning demand. As far as France is concerned, the UK comes well down the export pecking order: a third of organic wines made in France are exported to Germany, while we receive just 8 per cent of what they make.

Those 5456 hectares under vine produce 270,000 hectolitres (hl) of wine, of which 100,000 hl come from Languedoc-Roussillon in the south. Maybe you'd expect the Languedoc to produce the largest organic volume because it's the region that also produces the largest volume of France's non-organic wine. It contains a third of all France's vines, or, to put it another way, more than the total area under vine in the whole of the US. The Languedoc is the perfect place to make organic wine – hot and dry, a true Mediterranean climate.

Unfortunately this region must also take considerable responsibility for the EU wine lake. Despite all the organic efforts, the majority of production is mostly indifferent table wine from producers much more interested in a quick return, and the EU is anxious to reduce the wine lake by getting them to grub up vines and plant something different.

But what if these producers were encouraged to go for quality and convert to organic methods? Some truly excellent organic wines, such as Château de Caraguilhes, come from round here. And the Languedoc producers who focus on quality are cheerfully ignoring France's strict laws decreeing what can be made where (the appellation contrôllée or AC system, see below) and planting what suits them where it suits them and calling it country wine, vin de pays.

France, to harmonise with EU wine laws, differentiates between vin de table – table wine, basic, very little regulation apart from must be made of grapes, that sort of thing – and appellation contrôllée wine. This is the most tightly regulated level, setting down grape varieties to be planted, methods of pruning and training, and often going so far as to set down the date for commencement of harvest. The wines are supposed to be vetted by a national approval body, but in a bit of a scandal in 1996 it was revealed that over 97 per cent of wines submitted for approval go through on the nod. Not much control happening there, apparently.

What else? VDQS (Vin Delimité de Qualité Superieur) is an intermediate level below AC, and is now seen less and less often. Vin de pays is where most of the exciting work is happening in France, as it's the label chosen by innovative winemakers fed up with what they see as the unnecessary restrictions imposed on them by the AC system. This way they can plant what they like, how they like, and make a wine in any style they please.

I'm delighted to report that there's now an organic vin de pays, Viognier from Languedoc, coming to the UK (thank you, Vinceremos). This is good news because the planting there of Viognier, that luscious, fragrant, capricious, expensive grape, has transformed its availability and – more importantly – price. Once only grown in the northern Rhône – and highly priced – it's great that this grape is now reaching a wider audience. Let's hope the next edition of this book will be packed with Viognier recommendations.

Provence provides a further 20 per cent of France's organic wine – hot climate winning out again. By comparison, cooler (but still dry) Alsace accounts for a mere 1 per cent, and Burgundy for just 3 per cent of the national organic total. Though, of course, Burgundy is a region where quality predominates over quantity. And if you look at the proportion of organic vines to total vines in Burgundy in comparison to the proportion in France as a whole, a different picture emerges.

In France nationally, organic production has still to break the 1 per cent barrier, whereas 2 per cent of Burgundy growers farm organically, to make up that 3 per cent of the national total. That implies a greater-than-average awareness of, and commitment to, organic viticulture. Not surprising, I guess, in a region where so many have been concerned about the lifeless soil. Organic and, especially, biodynamic methods are the only means of restoring it to life.

Burgundy offers an excellent example of the minefield that awaits anyone trying to decipher the difference between organic certification and eco wines. All those small-scale peasant growers, making wine the way nature intended but who can't be doing with organising the certification process, aren't going to be able to (or don't want to) declare themselves organic on the label. Growers to watch out for here include Domaine Leroy and Domaine Leflaive (both biodynamic) and A&P de Villaine, all of whom make superb wine.

Further north, in the damp, misty Loire valley, Domaine Huet farm biodynamically and make a consistently good range of wines.

ITALY

Italy's organic acreage beats France's – they declared 5826 hectares (14,385 acres) in 1997. Add to that a stunning 10,500 hectares (nearly 26,000 acres) in conversion, and you have a force to be reckoned with of over 16,000 hectares (40,000 acres) in full organic production by 2000. Not unnaturally, given the climate, Sicily leads the field, with nearly 5000 hectares (12,000 acres) in total, but (in descending order) Puglia, Sardinia, Emilia-Romagna and Tuscany are all making good headway.

Italy has excellent climatic conditions for organic winemaking and I very much hope that it'll be taken up by the young, innovative winemakers who have done so much to inject life and interest into Italy's winemaking in recent years. It's a country much given to proud, idiosyncratic winemaking, with lots of complicated rules and nomenclatures that everyone seems happily to ignore. No reason to expect organic producers will be any different.

Italy is above all red wine country. The white wines, frankly, score pretty high in the CFDN stakes, but one of the most interesting things I've noticed, in completing this comprehensive trawl of worldwide organic wines, is how much flavour and zest the organic Italian whites have shown. Organic production really does seem to make a most pronounced difference with these wines.

Both reds and whites are reasonably well represented on the UK market. The organic specialists list several organic Italian producers, and the Edinburgh-based Italian importers Valvona and Crolla offer a range of eco wines.

GERMANY

As you might imagine, organic production in Germany is strictly controlled and monitored. One organic association, Naturland, has 17 estates with altogether over a million organic vines, grown on 250 hectares (617 acres). Another, the Federal Association for Ecological Viticulture, claims over 230 members, an encouraging number, cultivating a total of nearly 1000 hectares (2469 acres) of vines. They identify themselves under the name Ecovin. As in France, around 1 per cent of growers are following organic rules. You can see their rules and regulations on page 21.

A crucial feature of German organic winemaking is that organic growers can't chaptalise, i.e. add sugar to the fermenting grape juice to bring the alcohol content up a degree or two. In Germany, a country right on the edge of where you can grow grapes successfully, ripeness is queen and their whole appellation system is based on the amount of (naturally occurring) sugar in the resulting wine, whether or not there's any residual sugar left in the wine for you to taste.

German winemakers farming conventionally are allowed to chaptalise their lesser wines. The German quality ladder hops from Tafelwein (table wine, which can have sugar added), via QbA (Qualitätswein bestimmter Anbaugebiete), an intermediate level to which sugar can also be added, to the top run of QmP (Qualitätswein mit Prädikat). In this top category, wines are classified according to ripeness: from Kabinett, Spätlese, Auslese ... right on up to Trockenbeerenauslese, a wine made from individual berries shrivelled by fungal attack on the vine to unbelievable levels of ripeness, sweetness and general wonderful unctuousness.

Buying wine from organic German producers will at least mean you can be confident the 'sun in the bag' hasn't been added at any level. The other way round the sweetening issue in Germany is to add 'süssreserve', sweet reserve, which is grape juice still containing all its natural sugar that the yeast hasn't yet converted to alcohol. Organic producers, however, must abstain from adding sugar at any stage.

German society is far more advanced than the UK in terms of ecological awareness. All packaging now has to be returnable for recycling. When I lived in Frankfurt ten years ago, each block of flats already had three types of waste bin, where you could separate out glass and newspapers for recycling on your doorstep rather than having to lug them to the nearest bottle banks. Given the quantity of wine we all seemed to get through, to say nothing of the weight of British newspapers collected each Sunday from Frankfurt airport, this was quite a consideration.

German viticulture claims it offers the most advanced environmental protection in the world. With a classification system to match this commitment, we'll have a proposition we can understand – and will want to buy.

Demeter

The goddess of harvest lends her name to the international brand name given to certified biodynamic produce, be it food or wine. Sometimes producers who grow their grapes biodynamically use the Demeter logo, sometimes they don't, so its absence doesn't mean the wine isn't biodynamic. And indeed in certain countries, such as Germany and New Zealand, the Demeter certification bodies refuse to certify wines altogether. Rudolf Steiner, original impetus behind biodynamics, disapproved of alcohol as he felt it hindered spiritual growth. In France, however, and in most other countries, a more pragmatic view prevails and Demeter will certify wines.

Watch out too for the new certifying body Biodyvin, to which some of the top names in France have already signed up, with more due to follow.

AUSTRIA

With 621 hectares (1533 acres) under vine, Austria's organic production accounts for just 1.2 per cent of total winemaking. In this, viticulture seems to be lagging behind other areas of farming, where the proportion of organic farms is 8.3 per cent of the total. Austrian subsidy to organic grape growers amounts to around 320 ecu per hectare.

In the context of burgeoning support among Austrian consumers for organic produce, it is disappointing that one of the country's largest producers, Lenz Moser, has stopped producing organically in favour of Integrated Pest Management (see pages 24–25). On the other hand, Austria, which shares many winemaking practices with Germany, has yields running at half the average German levels, which is a Good Thing and means greater concentration in the glass. Maybe that's something Germany will focus on when it finally overhauls its wine law.

SPAIN

Spain has half as much land again under vine as France or Italy, making it the country with the most vineyards in the world, yet it is only the third most important producer of wine worldwide. This is because the climate is exceptionally dry but irrigation is banned, so yields come down to an average of just 25 hl per hectare.

Of Spain's 1.4 million hectares (3.5 million acres) of vines just 3120 hectares are farmed organically – and that includes both wine and table grapes. So you can see that, so far, things aren't wildly exciting for Spanish organics. In wine, anyway. You're eight times more likely to find organically grown olive oil (also worth supporting, of course). After joining the EU in 1986, along with Portugal, Spain has made huge strides in winemaking.

Like the rest of the EU, Spain has adopted a classification system based on getting more and more specific about region, moving from bottom-line table wine (vino de mesa) up to DO, Denominación de Origen. Like Topsy, this top-line appellation just 'growed and growed', so that now nearly half Spain's total vineyards are classified DO.

Spain is ideally placed to capitalise on the new demand for organic wine, as its hot, dry climate means that all the usual problems – botrytis, fungus, mildew (powdery and downy), are almost unheard-of. Drought is a major problem – overstressed vines don't produce, hence the dramatically low yields – but the EU bans irrigation. There are, however, licensed experiments being carried out in certain areas which are transforming them into far more productive wine regions, with yields comparable to the rest of Europe. Certainly the main retailers of organic wines are bullish about the new wines from Spain they're bringing on stream; they've identified an upsurge not just in availability but also quality, which is even more important.

PORTUGAL

This tiny country – less than 193 km (120 miles) wide and 579 km (360 miles) long – has widely varying climatic conditions, which is why it can produce both prickly, refreshing Vinho Verde and luscious rich, ripe port. In some parts of the country the hot dry conditions mean there is little need for spraying, so organic farming is something they could consider expanding. At present just 713 hectares (1760 acres) of organic grapes are grown here.

The Associacio Portuguese de Agriculture Biologic writes, delightfully: 'We cherish your interest in our country ... unfortunately our percentage of organic grape is quite low. Within the last six years there has been a slow increase in production (up from 103 hectares in 1993). As to producers imported to the UK, we're afraid there isn't any current data available.' Happily, Vinceremos have found one. And all the organic specialists offer organic port.

GREECE

Intending organic producers in Greece are much helped by a propitious climate. Rains come in winter and early spring but not in summer, so the hot dry Mediterranean conditions are ideal. Better understanding of vineyard management techniques, such as allowing the air to circulate in the leaf canopy, also help. And they're not short of sheep manure. It's harder to cultivate organically in areas such as Naoussa in Macedonia, where later harvests run the gauntlet of September rains or morning fog.

Greece has three certifying bodies (why so many?) approved by the EU. Winery names to look out for, some of whom are still in conversion to full organic status, are: Spiropoloulos, Antonopoulos, Katogi, Merkouri and Strofilia. Some of these have already found their way on to the shelves of Oddbins, Vinceremos and Vintage Roots.

CYPRUS

Any organic wine to be had in Cyprus? In a word: no!

EASTERN EUROPE

The old joke here is that they're mostly organic by default because these wineries, struggling to modernise themselves after emerging from Stalinism, can't afford the chemicals. Which, of course, is only partly true – massive international investment, with flying winemakers parachuting in, has led to lots of CFDN whites, and mass plantings of 'international' varieties of both red and white grapes such as Chardonnay and Cabernet Sauvignon.

The main focus of effort has been on improving winery hygiene, and on making sure that the vines planted were actually of the varieties stated (there were lots of weird and wonderful things growing out there). All this means that while quality was improving, the impetus to focus on organic production was lacking. This may well change, although judging by the 'intensive' farming philosophy of several of the major players in this region, swift moves seem unlikely. The first organic wines are starting to trickle through but it'll be a while before it's a flood.

THE UNITED STATES OF AMERICA

To put the words 'organic wine' on the label in the US involves severe legal restrictions. The wines must contain just ten parts per million of sulphites and be from certified vineyards. If they adhere to this level of sulphites, the catch-all term 'contains sulfites' (sulfites simply being the variant American spelling for our more cumbersome ph) can be left off the label.

The term 'made with organically grown grapes' on the other hand means that the grapes come from certified organic vineyards but that organic processing hasn't necessarily followed. In particular, the level of sulphites in these wines can be much higher.

The distinction between these regulations has a lot to do with the

Winemaker profile:
the Bonterra brand at Fetzer Vineyards, Mendocino County, California

One of the main reasons offered for the lack of organic conversions among the bigger players is that of economy of scale. Easy to go organic on a small scale, but imagine a manure heap big enough to feed 100 acres. So it's incredibly heartening to come across a company farming organically on a large scale, and making a commercial success of it. The example the Californian giant Fetzer set through its Bonterra brand is surely a potent convincer for medium to large companies who would like to move towards more earth- and human-friendly farming practices, but doubt that it can work on a large scale. Big can be beautiful: Fetzer has 810 hectares (2000 acres) of certified organic vineyards and plans to have every vineyard converted by 2005 – not just for Bonterra, but for all Fetzer wines.

The Fetzer family gave themselves a head start by settling in Mendocino county, 160 km (100 miles) north of San Francisco, where weather conditions – cold winters, dry summers – help things along nicely. In these conditions, downy mildew, scourge of European and Australian producers, is unheard-of, and they rarely have problems with grey rot.

Fetzer began looking at organic viticulture after the success of a five-acre organic/biodynamic kitchen garden they laid out in 1985. At the same time the state of California was planning to outlaw certain insecticides, and vineyard workers were ordered to wear full protective clothing when spraying. When it came to having to encase their workers in moon suits to work the earth, Fetzer decided to find another way. They took a 70-acre site, where some not-very-successful Sauvignon Blanc was planted, and began work.

The changeover began with compost: 'that's the fastest way to affect the soil – but conventional farmers ignore it,' notes Bonterra winemaker Bob Blue. 'It adds organic matter, loaded with fungus, which inoculates the soil and quickly produces a huge increase in earthworms. We feed the soil and the soil feeds the plant. A healthy plant withstands disease pressure, just like us.'

Then they sowed cover crops, which feed the soil and assist with insect control by providing predators, as well as pests, with a safe overwintering site. The predators are vital. 'If you plough the rows you have total monoculture, and the vineyard is quiet – there are no insects. So if bugs come in you have no choice but to spray.'

Redtail hawks, falcons and barn owls make short work of any invading rodents, but Bob admits defeat with deer and he fences in the vineyards to keep the little dears away from the ripening grapes. Plum trees ringing the vineyards also encourage the tiny parasitic wasps that prey on leafhoppers.

The company has made many moves towards self-sufficiency. It set up its own cooperage, for instance, building all the company's fermentation and maturation barrels, mostly from American oak from second-generation Mississippi forests – the ones planted after the first were cut down in the steamboat era. Only another five wineries in the world have taken things this far.

Many companies have mission statements. Here's an extract from Fetzer's list of its own 'environmental and social strategies' which notes some of its achievements in the last decade or so. Many other companies are working in this area, and I quote it to demonstrate just how you can find ways of minimising your company's impact on the world around you.

● Eliminate the need for capsules on bottles – use a more environmentally friendly wax seal. Bonterra print labels

on kenaf, a paperless hemp.
- Landfill dump fees cut by 86 per cent since 1991. The company now recycles everything from aluminium to oil in in-house recycling centres.
- Convert all stems and seeds from crushed grapes – 42,000 tons of them – into compost.
- Import cork direct from Portugal – the only US winery to do so, saving wasteful packaging (and around $8 per thousand corks).
- Reduce electricity consumption by $5000 a month. Investigate ways of capturing the carbon dioxide released during fermentation for re-use.

I'm not suggesting Fetzer are alone in pursuing these initiatives, because they're not; what's so good is to see a large winemaker adopting these practices (and the other good works, donations etc). Imagine what a difference it will make when all the other big wineries come on board.

structure of the industry in the US. In California, for instance, where most of the good news about American organics originates, far more grapes are grown organically than end up in bottles labelled as such. There are many organic growers who don't vinify their own grapes but sell them on to be processed elsewhere. And whereas in France most of the small growers not wishing to process their own production would be members of the local co-operative, in California they'll sell the grapes on to privately owned wineries. There, the chances are the grapes will slosh around in a vat with non-organically grown grapes, because the winemaker hasn't yet seen any point (financial or otherwise) in separating them out.

That seems bound to change as demand for organic wine continues to boom. Even now, the wine industry in California has more certified organic acreage than any other farm crop – in 1997 that was around 2 per cent of the state's wine grape acreage, 9281 acres

(3314 hectares). And, as elsewhere in the world, there are many wineries in California where grapes are grown organically but for whatever reason this is not stated on the label.

For both these reasons I believe we can expect to see marked growth in organic wines from California over the next year or two, as producers wake up to the goldmine growing on their doorstep. Maybe we'll see something of organic wines from Oregon and Washington, too. And even Canada (though not if they keep on putting their wines in transgenic winter jackets).

CHILE

Chile opened up to world wine markets in the early 1990s, following slowly on from the return to democracy in the 1980s. Between 1987 and 1993 Chile planted over 10,000 hectares (25,000 acres) of vines – and, almost uniquely in the world, these are ungrafted. The louse phylloxera devastated vineyards throughout the world in the late nineteenth century. The wine industry seemed doomed until someone came up with the idea of grafting *Vitis vinifera* (the wine grape we know and love) on to resistant rootstocks from hybrid American vines which produce grapes we wouldn't want to drink unless really desperate. But because Chile is geographically isolated – that long thin strip of land protected by the Andes – they grow ungrafted vines and don't have to worry about phylloxera. Or, because of the dry climate, about downy mildew either, although botrytis and powdery mildew make regular visitations.

I'm aware of only one organic Chilean wine, Viña Carmen. The number will increase, though, because many Chilean growers are switching from selling grapes to the big bodegas to vinifying their own production. This means some interesting, distinctive wines will emerge – and some will be organic. At the moment, of course, the argument about Chile's fresh, lively, unspoilt soils providing the basis for better wines still applies, but using chemicals will deaden it more with every succeeding vintage. Let's hope the progress being made in producing wines that are interesting to drink will be compounded by growing the grapes that make them organic.

ARGENTINA

The old indigenous style – tired and flabby – is dying out as the world's supermarket wine buyers focus their attention on encouraging Argentina to produce wines that will compete internationally. Hot dry climates and absence of phylloxera bode well for increasing organic production, but more skill in winemaking is still needed – important enough in conventional winemaking, vital where increased expertise is needed to produce successful organic wines. Vintage Roots have sourced a couple of Argentine reds, as have Vinceremos. Well worth seeking out.

AUSTRALIA

Australia's climate certainly favours organic production. Most grape-growing areas have low humidity, which means relatively little need for fungal and pest spraying even for those who feel compelled to reach for the squirter. They also like to keep leaf cover to a minimum, which allows the fruit more access to the sun, and because fertiliser promotes leaf growth, that's an obvious disincentive to using it.

But, despite all these natural advantages, there are only two organic wines from Australia widely found on British shelves, the Penfolds Clare Valley Chardonnay-Sauvignon Blanc, and their Shiraz-Cabernet. Glenara and Eden Ridge also crop up from time to time, as do Botobolar and Robinvale. But really, given all the interesting wine made there now, the helpful climate, and above all the influence Australia has on our drinking habits, I thought there would be more organic wine coming out of Oz. Cheryl Kemp, education co-ordinator for the Biodynamic Farming and Gardening Association of Australia, explains the current position. 'Yes, there is some biodynamic and organic activity here in viticulture. There has been a huge upsurge in wine grapes being planted here. Best part of it is that the newcomers are also interested in looking at growing without chemicals, so we are getting quite popular amongst that lot. We have about four established winemakers using biodynamics and many just starting out.

'Organic and biodynamic winemaking in Australia is still very much in the pioneering stage at present. We have one or two more experienced, but none yet that I would say have a real understanding of the forces that work with biodynamics. They still work at the level of what can solve what problem, rather than what are the forces working here, and how best can I balance them with biodynamics.'

Several estates are 'nearly' organic (is that like being nearly pregnant?), among them the widely available, 400-hectare (988-acre) Banrock Station estate. This belongs to BRL Hardy, one of Australia's major players. Banrock reduces its spraying to the minimum by utilising a version of IPM (see pages 24–25), and also looks to reduce sulphur use. As you might expect from a large commercial operation, winemaker Brett Fleming pointed out to me that the decision to reduce inputs in the vineyard is based primarily on commercial, not ecological, reasoning – the benefits include a reduced workload in the winery. However, why should we care? Whatever works. Maybe soon they'll take the final step and forgo sprays altogether. Let's hope so. We need more soft, easy-drinking, well-priced, widely available ranges like this.

NEW ZEALAND

James Millton, the organic and biodynamic winemaker much quoted in this book, is a leading proponent of organic and biodynamic winemaking in New Zealand. You'll also find Nelson Vineyards wine on sale in the UK. Nobody seems very certain about the level of organic production over there, a theme common to many of the smaller wine-producing nations. But just because there isn't much information available, doesn't mean it isn't happening. And fortunately for us there are people dedicating themselves to seeking out organic wines and bringing them all back home. The crisp, fresh, lively New Zealand whites are something organic drinkers could certainly do with more of, so watch this space. By the next edition we could well be reading about a success story here.

James Millton speaks for many small organic producers, not just in New Zealand, when he says: 'Organic farming is a sunrise industry; conventional farming, with its reliance on chemicals, is a sunset industry. People need to be able to look at flowers and grass, not scorched earth such as you see after land has been sprayed with, say, a pre-emergence herbicide, which prevents weed seeds from germinating.

'We need to alter our perceptions of what is tidy and untidy as regards weeds, economic and uneconomic, healthy and unhealthy. What's the point of New Zealand maintaining a good balance of payments through agriculture and horticulture exports if people's health is at risk from contaminated food and a polluted environment?'

SOUTH AFRICA

South Africa may produce a million tons of grapes a year, making it the world's seventh largest wine producer, but as a nation it prefers to drink beer. Nevertheless vineyard activity is frenetic, grubbing up the old vines that mostly made the base wine for brandy and replanting with the ubiquitous international varieties.

The wines now emerging from South Africa are softer and fruitier than before. New areas are being planted; more modern winery practices adopted. One of the new ideas being implemented is the Integrated Production of Wine – IPW (see pages 26–27). This focuses on environmental conservation issues and is therefore a Good Thing, particularly as South African wine giant KWV (Co-operative Growers Association, the former state co-operative) has signed up to the programme. But it still stops short of full adoption of organic practice, which is a shame.

Meanwhile, two certified organic winemakers import to the UK: Sonop Wine Farm, who sell Cabernet Sauvignon and Pinotage (South Africa's speciality grape) through Vintage Roots; and Jordan, based in Stellenbosch, whose wines are available through Christopher Piper Wines in Devon.

ENGLAND

There are a couple of organic vineyards operating in England: Avalon near Glastonbury, and Sedlescombe in East Sussex. Both sell their wines from the farm gate but at time of writing the wines weren't available elsewhere, so I haven't included their wines in the review section. I'm aware of at least one other English vineyard hoping to convert to organic production, though, so maybe by the next edition the picture will look a little rosier. Meanwhile both of these estates can offer a pleasant day out and a chance to buy organic direct from the producer.

SWITZERLAND

It appears nobody from Switzerland who makes organic wine exports it to the UK. Which is probably just as well, really.

LEBANON

Chateau Musar is well known to lovers of red Leb, coming as it does from vineyards in the Lebanese Bekaa valley within shelling distance of Beirut. Some years it was almost impossible to get the harvest in under the bombardment. Yet, year after year, Serge Hochar brought his wine in and it's gorgeous. See page 119.

Roberson's Wine Merchants in London (see page 119w) have a remarkable stretch of vintages for Musar, and if you have the opportunity to indulge yourself it would be fun to buy a few and try what the trade calls a 'vertical tasting'. This has nothing to do with the condition you need to be in to participate, but means you line up wines from several vintages from the same property to see how it develops over time. And it can really be quite instructive.

8
WHO TO BUY FROM
AND HOW TO BUY WITH CONFIDENCE

HOW WAS THE list of organic, biodynamic and eco wines in the following chapter put together? And how did I find out who sold them? I faxed or e-mailed every UK wine retailer and wholesaler I could find – several hundred in total. Some of them really embraced the concept of the book and went away and researched their entire wine list, sending extensive questionnaires to every producer. Others scoffed at the very idea. Still others ignored the invitation. What's here is the fruit of that research. There are bound to be omissions, and I apologise in advance for errors. I do ask, though, if you would be kinder to me than was the man who, outraged by the fact that a well-known newspaper wine reviewer had under-quoted the price of a wine by 20p, rang up to berate him.

I deliberately cast the net as widely as possible so that you have the means to support local independents and mail-order specialists should you so choose. They are, after all, the ones making the most innovation in the way organic wines are brought before us.

We buy most of our wine from supermarkets: but if we want a wide selection of organic wines, we're going to have to look elsewhere. Sainsbury's, for instance, at the time of going to press, stocked just three certified wines, and expressed no knowledge of which others on their shelves might be produced according to organic principles. Asda offer just two generic organic wines. Morrisons didn't have any.

Things do change rapidly. Supermarkets have already woken up to the increasing demand, but, of course, these things take time. A more detailed note of individual supermarket policies follows, together with how to contact them if you feel like lobbying to encourage more organic wines on to their lists.

Certain specialist merchants will offer you much, much more, however. Did you know there were several mail-order companies who specialise in organic wines? It's an unaccountably well-kept secret. They list several hundred wines between them; they'll deliver to your door; they'll also sell you organic beer, spirits, juices, olive oil, chocolate ... cornucopia time. The other thing is, these guys haven't just opened up overnight and jumped on the bandwagon. They've been going for years – in fact they all opened up within a few months of each other in the late 1980s, around the time of the first upswing in interest in organic wine. They kept going through lean times when they must have felt they were swimming against the tide of public opinion. Now that the tide has turned they must be very happy people (and their brochures are getting shinier too).

The specialists believe organic wine will remain a niche market, largely because of the small volumes produced by many of their suppliers. Supermarkets can't muscle in and dominate the market in the way they can with conventional wines because the volumes they need to get wine on shelves in all their outlets simply aren't there. Though that might change in the next five years as demand grows and more growers convert to organic methods.

SUPERMARKETS VERSUS SPECIALISTS

There are many ways in which specialist merchants score over the supermarkets. If, like me, you don't have a car, clanking carrier bags full of glass bottles are a slog to lug back from the supermarket. And many wine shop staff turn up their finely tuned noses at dropping off a single case. Try mail order instead. They'll put together cases according to your price range and taste preferences and, joy of joys, you don't have to cart it home.

Many other merchants, while not focusing exclusively on certified organic producers, carry a decent selection of organic, biodynamic or eco wines. T&W Wines in Norfolk put particular emphasis on biodynamic producers, devoting a two-page spread in the latest brochure to explaining the arcane details of biodynamic practice. La Reserve, in London, also emphasises the virtues of biodynamic wines.

It's good advice to put yourself in the hands of a specialist: it's also worth putting pressure on supermarkets to stock more of the wines you want. Too many wines sold by supermarkets are produced to hit a price point, where the most valued elements are consistency (so the consumer knows what they're getting, year in year out) and stability (so the supermarket isn't bothered by customers bringing unstable 'off' wines back and demanding a refund).

Cost – is there any reason for it to be higher?

It's certainly true that organic wines appear to have a price premium, although it's not as grotesque a contrast as between organic and conventionally grown fruit and veg. Organic vegetable growers labour under the severe disadvantage of absence of government subsidy. I'm sure we'd have cheaper organic produce in the twinkling of an eye if the government funded organic growers in the way it funds intensive, chemical-based agriculture. There's no equivalent subsidy for winemaking, so at least there's a level playing field between conventional and organic wine, as far as financial competitiveness is concerned.

But if you grow organic, and aren't going to reach for the sprays if things go badly wrong, you risk losing a proportion of your crop – indeed, in severe cases, all of it. Organic viticulture can involve making some tough decisions. And, of course, in business terms, organic and biodynamic grape growing is more costly because it's far more labour-intensive. Processes that one worker and a spray machine would carry out under a conventional regime need to be done by lots of humans, working to an older, gentler rhythm. However, the cost of this extra labour is offset by the fact that organic producers are no longer lining the pockets of the big chemical companies.

Another reason for the higher price of organic wines is yield, the weight of grapes you allow the vines to produce per acre or hectare. Chemical fertilisers encourage growth, so the vines will produce more abundant crops of grapes; but, of course, there's only so much flavour that each vine can produce. There's an equation here, a trade-off between quantity and quality. Some producers (both organic and conventional) will take the labour-intensive step of conducting a 'green harvest' in early summer. This involves going through the vineyards, assessing how many tiny bunches of grapes each vine has produced, and cutting off the excess production.

Thus, at a snip, yields drop by 10 per cent or more, and the neighbours will probably think you're barking. But, come harvest, you'll smile sweetly on tasting the resulting wine. There may be less of it but the concentration of flavour will beat the quantity-driven neighbours hollow, and the improved quality will command a premium price.

This applies equally to organic and conventional producers – here the common denominator is an obsession with quality. If you come across a wine which demands a significantly higher price than others from the same place or appellation, consider the reason why. Sometimes it's fashion; sometimes the estate has been over-praised by wine writers and hiked its prices accordingly; but sometimes it's because it's worth it. If producers are making better wine with cleaner, clearer flavours because they're farming organically or biodynamically and making the wine with respect, they'll have produced a far better product, one which can command a much higher price. It's no secret that the world's finest estates farm organically, even if they don't admit to it. It's certainly worth considering taking the plunge and buying a bottle, to see for yourself whether or not the wine has that kind of value.

Another reason organic wines seem expensive in the high street is that they're mostly imported by specialist 'middle-persons'. The retailers – wholefood shops, for instance – can't compete on price with the supermarkets who are importing the wines directly and putting them straight on the shelves, largely avoiding wholesalers. That third element in the chain can put costs up. Another good reason for buying mail order, I guess.

DO YOU GET WHAT YOU PAY FOR?

The sad fact is that if your wine cost under, say, £3.50 a bottle, it has almost certainly been produced by winemakers and importers playing safe. In wine we don't necessarily get what we pay for – there's too much of a fashion element in modern wine-buying for that. There's still too much snobbery, too many once-magnificent winemaking names now trading emptily on their reputation, for us to be sure that it's always money well spent. But most of the wines in the following pages offer reasonable to excellent value for money. And they've been made honestly, emphasising the place from where they came, the grape variety and the vagaries of that year's weather. The wine has, as far as possible, been allowed to speak for itself with minimum intervention from man or woman.

DECODING THE LABEL

The safest, easiest, most reliable way to buy organic wine is to look for the word 'organic' somewhere on the label. You may see the bald statement 'organic wine'. You may see the more laborious, but accurate, 'wine made from organically grown grapes'. You may see the certifying body's name or logo. 'Terre et Vie', 'Nature et Progres' are two of the French certifying bodies. 'Ecocert' is another. Our own Soil Association name may appear too. For biodynamic wines, the certifying body Demeter, in its distinctive typeface (confusingly also used by the National Westminster Bank) guarantees biodynamic status.

But, as we've already seen, absence of the word 'organic' on the label is no proof that the wine within wasn't made according to organic principles. Then we have to turn detective and look for little clues. 'Unfiltered', for instance. If someone puts that on the label it's no indicator of organic status, but it does indicate the wine was made by someone who didn't want to strip its heart out. With the word 'unfiltered' the producer wants to alert you to the possibility of sediment lurking at the bottom of the bottle. 'Unfiltered' warns you to pour with care, and leave the dregs in the bottle, or maybe even decant the wine. At the very least, this word tells you that the wine is more natural than a filtered one.

Another small clue comes with certain Californian wines. By law, all wines in the US must carry the warning label 'contains sulfites'. This is supposed to be a warning to asthmatics, who may react to the sulphur in wines (especially if they drink in unfeasibly large quantities). Organic wines, however, have lower maximum sulphur levels; and Californian wines containing under 10 parts per million of sulphur do not need to carry that labelling. So a warning-free Californian wine is probably organic.

Now for export to us, of course, some producers will leave off the sulphites warning because it's not a legal requirement here, so its absence doesn't prove anything. But its presence can indicate to us that other chemicals may well have been used.

Any general waffle on labels about respecting nature and the environment could well be just that: feelgood stuff, not backed up by certification or hard evidence. By all means believe it, but it doesn't prove anything. Claims to use 'traditional methods' may actually refer to the local tradition of spraying the vines into knock-kneed submission every summer. You can't get away from the fact that the only way to be absolutely certain of a wine's organic status is for it to be certified. Nor can you get away from the fact that certified organic status is not labelled as such by some producers. So use this book instead to find the wines that are made to organic principles.

ORGANIC SPECIALISTS

VINTAGE ROOTS
FREEPOST, Reading, Berkshire RG2 9ZZ
Freephone: 0800 980 4992
Phone: 0118 976 1999
Fax: 0118 976 1998
Website: (accepts online orders) www.vintageroots.co.uk

The largest of the three specialists, with over 200 wines listed, Vintage Roots reflect a trend when they report that their turnover is now more than double what it was five years ago. Founders Lance Pigott and Neil Palmer came across their first organic vineyards while in France one year for the fruit harvest. Twentysomethings looking for something to do, they set up shop in November 1986, importing just ten wines direct from the vineyards. Everything sold out that Christmas and business kept on growing. In the late 1980s it grew with the 'Green Revolution' but then bottomed out in the early 1990s with the recession. A year or two later it started increasing again and is blossoming.

Their average bottle price is between £4 and £6 but that average is rising. They sell direct to the public via their mail-order service and to other organic companies such as Organics Direct and the Fresh Food Co who offer wine as well as food. As you become expert in the organic wine selections available you'll be able to walk into any wholefood shop, look at the dozen or so wines they have on sale, and tell at once whether they were supplied by Vintage Roots or Vinceremos (see next page).

Vintage Roots' list is wide-ranging. Plenty from France, as you might expect, but also a lively selection from Italy. Little from Germany (sadly, few German organic wines are imported by anyone), but an expanding range from Spain. More recherché items include fruit wines and mead, while they'll also accommodate requests for liqueurs and spirits, beer, cider, juice, and even oils and vinegars. They offer various selection cases as starter ideas, or will make up a case mixed to suit what you want – just name your price level. I also noticed while I was tasting there that each new customer got a bar of organic chocolate with their first order. Nice touch. Just don't eat it with the wine ...

VINCEREMOS
19 New Street, Leeds LS18 4BH
Phone: 0113 205 4545
Fax: 0113 205 4546
e-mail: info@vinceremos.co.uk
Website: www.vinceremos.co.uk

Vinceremos began life on an Aeroflot flight. Founder Jerry Lockspeiser, on holiday to mark the end of his student days, drank Russian vodka and wine on the plane home, like you do if you want to forget you're travelling Aeroflot.

He liked what he drank, and set up a buying group for friends, as a hobby. That grew into a business selling unusual products such as Bulgarian wine. (This was a few years ago, remember. In 1985 a lot of things seemed novel that are commonplace now. Pit closures. Dire Straits. New Labour.)

Jerry found sales of organic wine took off in a major way, expanding to fill the void created by the fact that the rest of the world caught up with Bulgarian wine and soon there were no more unusual products to be found. Like Vintage Roots, Vinceremos experienced rapid growth until the recession pulled the rug. Lean times followed, but life picked up again in 1993. Steady growth to 1997 was then leapfrogged by the acceleration we've seen in all areas of organic production, and understandable reaction to fears about the safety of our food and drink.

Jem Gardener, who runs Vinceremos, reckons that organic wines express the character of a wine's terroir more truly, though he too points to the onus organic practices put on the winemaker to do a really excellent job. 'Organic winemakers can't take the short-cuts that others can. I've tasted too many appalling organic wines, made without enough skill.'

Their list of around 170 wines also majors on France (currently their house white is made by Richard Doughty from Bergerac, knocking spots off just about everything else in the price range – hurry, it's going fast) and they carry a full range from James Millton in New Zealand. There's some powerful stuff from Australia too. Again, they'll offer mead, cider, beer, juices, olive oil and spirits – including, as you may expect since that's where it all started, seven Russian vodkas (though these aren't organic). There are two verified organic spirits: Calvados VSOP and Da Mhile malt whisky.

Ask about low sulphur wines if you have a problem with sulphur – they should be able to point you towards the lower-sulphur wines on the list.

Historical note: 'Vinceremos' started life as a pun on the Chilean revolutionary slogan 'Venceremos' – we will win – a fact self-evident to every 1970s student firebrand and completely mystifying to everyone else. Must have seemed like a good idea at the time – I really like it – but as Jem Gardener ruefully told me: 'We spend [waste?] a lot of time explaining this to people.'

HENRY DOUBLEDAY RESEARCH ASSOCIATION (HDRA)
19 New Street, Leeds LS18 4BH
Phone: (wine orders) 0113 205 4558
e-mail: hdrawine@bottlegreen.com

The HDRA supports all aspects of organics, including the sale of organic wine. This is on offer through their shop at Ryton Organic Gardens near Coventry, and also via mail order to HDRA members. With over 60 organic wines on sale in the shop, this has to be about the largest UK organic retail outlet. The mail-order club offers around 170 wines, and is administered by Vinceremos.

Prices are the same as those offered by Vinceremos, but the added incentive here is that a percentage of the retail price will be diverted towards supporting the HDRA's research programme. And since they're responsible for some of the most innovative and useful research available on organic gardening this is well worth supporting. Join now ... (no, really, I don't get a percentage, how could you think such a thing?).

HDRA members receive such useful things as an organic seed catalogue and a regular newsletter, so if you're at all interested in organic gardening or supporting sustainable agriculture this is a worthwhile organisation to join. They're also heavily committed to the cause of organic wine. Jackie Gear, who runs the HDRA, initiated the National Organic Food and Wine Fair that ran at Ryton for six years. Some of my first encounters with organic wines took place there, when I was a judge for their Organic Wine Challenge. The time is ripe to reconstitute those awards, I think!

THE ORGANIC WINE COMPANY
PO Box 81, High Wycombe, Bucks HP13 5QN
Phone/fax: 01494 446557

This company took their first order in 1986. They benefited from the surge of interest in the late 1980s, and supplied lots of samples to supermarkets which, owner Tony Mason claims, then went and bought direct, cutting his company out of the picture.

In disgust he set up an operation in the US, which now accounts for an increasing part of the company's business. He's keen to export substantial volumes to the US because 'it deprives the UK supermarkets of availability. I want to limit the choice, because strategically that's good for us. We can then continue to offer a good range of wines and the supermarkets are still scrabbling around for eight different labels.' I must have look puzzled, because he explained further: 'You see, I suspect you and I are coming at this from a slightly different angle. You want to make available to the public the widest possible choice through the easiest possible channel. I don't.'

One of the most interesting things this company does is offer a trip across the channel a couple of times a year. They set off in a minibus, towing a trailer, at the crack of dawn and each traveller can bring back up to ten cases at French duty rates from their depot near Calais. These events are booked up months in advance, and given the savings involved that's hardly surprising.

There are a few question marks in my mind about this operation, however. One is simply the fact that there isn't a separate fax line, which always makes me leap to the conclusion that a company is very small. Secondly, their brochure is a small A5 black-and-white affair on standard photocopy paper which indeed looks as though it might have been photocopied rather than printed, with all the cost savings that brings. The other two organic specialists have obviously taken some trouble over brochure design and execution. And this is also one of those irritating brochures that contains marginal abbreviations but no easily discovered key. Thirdly, their focus on the US market – is it at the expense of us at home?

But my overriding concern is the quality and standard of the wines. I'm sure they must have many satisfied customers, or they wouldn't still be in business but I found several of the wines I was given to taste were over the hill. Two of the wines I tasted were ones where Mason stocks several vintages. In both cases the oldest available vintage had been opened for me to taste and both of these had seen better days. With both wines his verdict was: 'Yes, I think that'll be going in a bin-end special offer.' So does he not know which of his wines are showing well and which aren't? Again, why put on a wine in that condition for a writer to taste? Were I not such an easygoing, charitable soul I'd say he was trying to stitch me up.

INDEPENDENT WINE MERCHANTS

PLANET ORGANIC
42 Westbourne Grove, London W2 5SH
Phone: 0171 221 7171

A pioneering supermarket, Planet Organic sells only organic products. They stock everything from fresh meat (including fillet steak at a whopping £39.90 per kilo) and bread to spices and wine. There's even a juice bar. The range of wines offered is extensive, and some feature in this book. Just watch the mark-ups, which are variable and sometimes quite high compared to other sources, such as mail-order specialists Vinceremos and Vintage Roots.

THE FRESH FOOD CO – ORGANIC NATION
Phone: 0181 969 0351
Website: www.freshfood.co.uk

This is one-stop organic shopping, delivered to your door. The Fresh Food Co operates a nationwide delivery service of over 200 wines, plus beers, spirits and 'fresh and dry' organic foods. You can order online or by phone. They stock mainly wines from Vintage Roots, at roughly similar prices.

ADNAMS
Sole Bay Brewery, Southwold, Suffolk IP18 6JW
Phone: 01502 727200
Fax: 01502 727201
e-mail: info@adnams.co.uk

Simon Loftus has single-handedly built up the wine operation based at Adnams brewery over the last 20 years or so, and is passionately devoted to 'unmucked-about-with' wines, as the quotes scattered throughout this book show. His list contains many hidden eco gems, several of which are reviewed in the following chapter, and although Adnams don't specialise in organic wines, they champion unfiltered, chemical-free wine. Worth investigating.

T&W WINES

51 King Street, Thetford, Norfolk IP24 2AU
Phone: 01842 765646
Fax: 01842 766407
Website: www.tw-wines.co.uk

Trevor Hughes set up T&W Wines over 20 years ago after a successful career as hotelier, and it's significant that a large part of his business is still done through the UK's top-rated restaurants. However, he has a thriving private client list, both through the Thetford shop and nationally via mail order. I first fell over Trevor five years ago when he berated me for writing books that encouraged people to buy wine direct from winemakers rather than in the UK (from him!). We're marginally more civil to each other these days and I take my hat off to him for the support he gives the biodynamic winemakers. He has even offered to put together a special introductory tasting case of his biodynamic products for readers of this book, so give the shop a ring if you're interested.

ROBERSON WINE MERCHANTS

348 Kensington High Street, London W14 8NS
Phone: 0171 371 2121
Fax: 0171 371 4010
e-mail: wines@roberson.co.uk
Website: www.roberson.co.uk

Roberson have one of the most stylish and idiosyncratically dressed showrooms I've ever seen – all strangely wrought shapes and improbable pillars. Very postmodern, great fun, but more to the point it's a receptacle for some truly wonderful wines. And, sensibly, they've siphoned off all the organic wines and made a special display of them because customers were so keen to know what was organic. Excellent; my kind of wine merchant. They have really good-quality wines from all over the world. If you're a fan of Serge Hochar, for instance, the incredibly brave owner and winemaker at

Chateau Musar in the Lebanon, who pulled a harvest in year after year under the shelling of nearby Beirut and who farms organically, you can find a brilliant selection of vintages here.

VALVONA AND CROLLA
19 Elm Row, Edinburgh EH7 4AA
Phone: 0131 556 6066
Fax: 0131 556 1668
e-mail: sales@valvonacrolla.co.uk

Valvona and Crolla, the splendid Italian wine specialists based in Edinburgh, ran with the idea of this book wholeheartedly. They faxed every single producer on their wine list with my definition of what constitutes an organic wine, and came back to me with details. The wines from Valvona and Crolla that I've listed in the following chapter are eco rather than certified organic, and therefore can't be taken quite as literally as those with the piece of paper to prove it. Especially as Italian producers have a propensity to tell you whatever it is they think you want to hear. Nevertheless, this research has opened up a new vista of eco Italian wines from small and quirky producers.

CHRISTOPHER PIPER WINES
1 Silver Street, Ottery St Mary, Devon EX11 1DB
Phone: 01404 814139
Fax: 01404 812100

Another merchant now avidly questioning all suppliers about their organic status, Christopher Piper's organisation admirably serves the entire West Country with a weekly delivery service. At present they've only identified a few organic/eco wines, but it won't be long before they have a complete picture of who's making the wines we want to drink. Merchants who have bothered to undertake this thorough an audit deserve encouragement.

THE WINERY
4 Clifton Road, London W9 1SS
Phone: 0171 286 6475
Fax: 0171 286 2733

Tucked away in smart Maida Vale, this shop is kitted out in the garb of the nineteenth-century chemist which it once was, right down to the open fire burning in a corner (fuelled by gas today, alas). This is a high-end selection, with next to nothing under a fiver, but with a decidedly unsnooty and very helpful staff. Definitely a place to come for user-friendly assistance. A year ago they put their toes in the importing pond for the first time; now they wish they'd done it years ago. Around 20 per cent of the wines they import are organic and the percentage is rising.

SUPERMARKETS

SAINSBURY'S
Customer helpline: 0800 636262
Website: www.sainsbury's.co.uk

The sea-change in Sainsbury's organic policy is terrific. All over the place, their blue organic logo is draped over the shelves advertising itself. It actually makes shopping much swifter, because everything you want is grouped together.

Sainsbury's say they plan to expand their organic wine range (just as well – it's a mere three wines at the moment) and they promise to merchandise them in the wine aisle flagged up as organic wines. That'll be helpful. They also promise to eliminate all genetically modified organisms, including from wine, and to that end are part of a consortium dedicated to sourcing non-GM foods which also includes Marks and Spencer.

Their comment on the state of the market: 'Organic wine sales will continue to rise due to an increase in customer awareness.

Sainsbury's plan to support this by introducing more organic wines and merchandising all organic wines together.'

TESCO
Customer service helpline: 0800 505555
Website: www.tesco.co.uk

Tesco make a much bigger fist of their organic selection, scoring well over the half dozen in a satisfyingly broad price band – £4.29 to £14.99. They say demand for organic wine is buoyant, although it is still a small part of their business. Apart from widely available favourites such as Bonterra and Millton Vineyards, there are own-label French and Italian organics, plus a white from Hungary – a rare sighting. Where stores are legally allowed to do so, they are displaying the organic wines alongside organic groceries, which I do think is a helpful move. More identification issues are to be resolved by issuing organic wines with collaretes (isn't that a funny word?).

MARKS & SPENCER
Phone: (general) 0171 935 4422; (complaints) 0171 268 1234

Having been wrong-footed in a major way over organic produce, Marks and Spencer currently have just one organic wine. They aim to introduce two or three more to the range soon, which is progress, but I do exhort you to watch the prices like a hawk, because if the example of their bread pricing is anything to go by, organic wine buyers will be in danger of getting a raw deal.

If you buy organic bread in a supermarket you'll expect to pay between 85p and 99p for an 800 g organic wholemeal. Marks and Spencer, on the other hand, want 99p for a mere 400 g loaf. Who in their right mind is going to pay that? Not you, I hope. So watch out for what they charge for wine. If it's 'what the market will bear' go elsewhere. Though not, of course, before making your views known. They've even set up a special complaints line – very handy.

SAFEWAY
Phone: 01622 712000

Safeway were once pioneers of all things organic, even sponsoring the Organic Wine Challenge held at the HDRA's headquarters in Ryton until a few years ago. Their current range offers four organic wines, a quartet from the cheaper end of the market – and full of honest flavour. I hope they'll find a few more.

ASDA
Phone: 0500 100055

Asda currently stock two organic wines and do not seem to have any strong desire to increase this. They have a website, *www.asda.co.uk,* which at present contains no information on wine.

WAITROSE
Phone: (wine direct) 0800 188881
Website: www.waitrose-direct.co.uk

Waitrose are showing a commendable attitude to all things organic, including wine. At the moment they list a broad range of 11 organic wines, all nicely flagged up on the shelf labels.

CO-OP
Customer relations hotline: 0800 317827
Website: www.co-op.co.uk (you can order mixed cases online)

The Co-op shows an admirable willingness to grasp the nettle of more informed customer choice, even to the extent of being prepared to break labelling laws. It's illegal to state ingredients, such as sulphur levels, on wine labels; all power to the Co-op for recognising the ludicrousness of not being allowed to tell us what we need to know.

HIGH STREET CHAINS

ODDBINS
Mail order: 0870 601 0015
Website under construction: http://www.oddbins.co.uk

As exemplary in this as in most other aspects of their retailing, Oddbins have been seeking out organic-status wines, even if not fully certified. Recently they've made forays into Greece, where some particularly exciting winemaking innovations are taking place, and the results can be found on the shelves. Oddbins staff are full of enthusiasm for the product and, these days, seem to be considerably less bumptious, which makes buying there so much more pleasant. (The Canterbury Westgate branch is first-rate.)

THRESHER/VICTORIA WINE
Phone: 01707 328244

A very patchy organisation, struggling to find an identity after this huge merger. The press office is particularly hard to get anything out of, and branches seem variable both in terms of stock carried and level of training among staff. A few organic wines are stocked, but company policy on the future development of the sector seems unclear. And after one person told me about several organic wines, the next time I rang the press office another person told me they weren't organic after all. Oh well. At the moment all you can find there is Bonterra; but the Alsace wines of Zind-Humbrecht, long sold by Wine Rack, are converting to biodynamics. Just don't tell the press office.

MAJESTIC
Phone: 01923 298200
Mail order and delivery service: 01727 847935
Website: www.majestic.co.uk

Majestic have around a dozen organic wines starting with a vin de pays de Vaucluse blanc for all of £2.99. They say if customers start demanding more organic wines then they'll react to that demand. So, it's up to you, start demanding. A real plus point for Majestic is their free nationwide delivery service. Contact your nearest branch or use the number above.

9
Bringing it all back home:
all the wine that's fit to drink (and some that isn't)

Whites under £5

France

1996 Château Côtes des Caris
Bordeaux Blanc Sec
Christian Guichard
Organic Wine Company £3.99
Certified organic, vegan
Fresh, clean, aromatic nose, reasonable concentration, well balanced and with refreshing acidity (in other words, CFDN? How can you think such a thing!). Well made and reasonably priced. Hey, it's the first review, I'm being polite.

1997 French Organic Wine
Vinceremos, HDRA £4.29
Certified organic
Now this . . . Vinceremos managed to persuade Bergerac's Richard Doughty to produce their house white last year, a brilliant move because this wine knocks most of the competition into a cocked hat.

It has aromas that reach out of the glass and grab you by the throat. It has buttery ripe fruit on the palate. It has terrific concentration, good structure and more sheer taste than wines of twice the price. And if it doesn't sell out rapidly I shall be very surprised.

1997 BORDEAUX
Château Vieux Georget
Vinceremos, HDRA £4.29
Certified organic, vegan
From his small chateau south of Bordeaux, Jean da Fré makes this wine from a blend of classic Bordeaux white varieties: Sémillon, Sauvignon and Muscadelle. A nose of ripe exotic fruit, good fresh acidity, well balanced in the mouth. Not hugely characterful but what do you expect from round here? Honest and lively.

1997 VIN DE PAYS D'OC, SAUVIGNON
Domaine de la Grangette
Organic Wine Company £4.39
Certified organic
Quite lively in the mouth, this, refreshing and buzzing with some grassy Sauvignon flavours.

1998 MARSANNE
Vin de Pays de l'Hérault,
Domaine de Petit Roubié
Vintage Roots £4.75
Certified organic, vegan
Lively, fresh wine with hints of lemon and grapefruit. It has a lovely bite to it, perfect for cutting through a rich, creamy dish of fish or chicken.

1997 PICPOUL DE PINET
Domaine de Petit Roubié
Vinceremos, HDRA £4.79; Organic Wine Company £4.69
Certified organic, vegan

An unexpectedly creamy nose and reasonable levels of fruit make this refreshing, unpretentious summer drinking but not much in the way of winter comfort. Picpoul is the grape, Pinet the southern French village down near the Mediterranean. It's a tartly acidic grape ('picpoul' was said to describe the puckered-up face you pulled on tasting it) and once upon a time it all just swilled into the base-wine tanks for vermouth – the Noilly Prat factory is just down the road. Now, however, the wine is made with more TLC and offered for what it is: light, refreshing, easy drinking.

1998 BLANC DE BRAU
Vin de Pays de l'Aude,
Domaine de Brau
Vintage Roots £4.85
Certified organic, vegan
From Wenny and Gabriel Tari's estate near Carcassonne, this charming mix of Chardonnay and Roussanne has an elegance and style way beyond its price.

1997 ENTRE-DEUX-MERS
Château la Blanquerie
Vinceremos, HDRA £4.89
Certified organic, vegan
The two seas the name refers to are actually rivers in Bordeaux – Garonne and Dordogne – and the wines are made entre the deux. It's a byword for bone-dry whites and this is no exception: light and fresh. CFDN, if I'm honest.

1997 ENTRE-DEUX-MERS
Domaine du Bourdieu
Vinceremos, HDRA £4.99
Certified organic, vegan
Ten pence doesn't make a ha'p'orth of difference between these two – another crisp, fresh, dry neutral wine which won't charm the pants off anyone but which will taste rather fine if eating fish outdoors on a summer's evening.

1998 Vin de Pays Des Côtes de Thongue, Sauvignon Blanc
Domaine Bassac
Vintage Roots £4.99
Certified organic, vegetarian
This wine packs a punch – a whopping 14 per cent alcohol, which gives it a very powerful mouth feel. Don't knock it back in hot sun, if we get any. Intense Sauvignon Blanc character, much richer than the cool Loire valley style; pungent gooseberries and grassiness.

1998/9 Biodynamic Blanc
Fiefs Vendeens
Vintage Roots £4.99
Biodynamic, vegan
A big, assertive label tells you exactly what you're getting, no messing. The one thing it doesn't tell you is where on earth the Fiefs Vendeens are (not a million miles from Poitiers). The nose is full of light floral notes, and in the mouth you'll notice some residual sugar giving it a lightly off-dry taste; but although this seems less than heavyweight, the finish lasts longer than you'd expect. As a basic, generic, house-wine sort of style, this has a lot going for it.

1998 Vin de Pays du Gard, Chardonnay
Domaine Costeplane
Vintage Roots £4.99
Certified organic, vegan
More a summer slurp than a winter comforter, this pale wine from the south of France has refreshing acidity and recognisable Chardonnay character (just) – ripe, buttery fruit.

1998 Touraine Sauvignon
Domaine de Pontcher
Majestic £4.99
Converting to biodynamic
Here we have a very clear, clean example of Loire Sauvignon

Blanc: a crisp gooseberry nose, and a light-bodied, juicy wine in the mouth, with plenty of acidity and zippy fruit. Organic wines are often said to express the character of the fruit and the region more clearly than conventional wines. This wine, from an estate taking organics very seriously, is a prime example. Touraine suffers from being the poor relation of its better-known neighbour Sancerre, so it often offers better value, as in this case.

ITALY

1998 SOLATIO BIANCO
Perlage
Vinceremos, HDRA £3.99
Certified organic, vegan
A light, fresh Italian number, from local varieties, with a typical aromatic nose, crisp appley, spicy fruit, and good acidity. Chill this well and serve outside in summer: crisp and refreshing.

1998 SERENEL FRIZZANTE
Bettili
Vintage Roots £4.45
Certified organic, vegan
Gently sparkling, with tangy bitter cherry fruit. Not much substance but fun for a picnic.

1998 CHARDONNAY
Perlage
Vinceremos, HDRA £4.69
Certified organic, vegan
Nice deep colour and plenty of good rich buttery Chardonnay flavour here. Input from Australian winemaker Steve Hagen resulted in a typical clean, fruit-driven Aussie style which gives this Italian white some extra punch.

1997 BIANCO DI CUSTOZA
Ottomarzo
Vinceremos, HDRA £4.99
Certified organic
Bianco di Custoza suffers from being close to Soave, as it's often overshadowed by its more famous neighbour. And, of course, neither wine is known for being big on personality. This wine also suffers from the Italian penchant for neutral whites; but it's still fresh and juicy, with lively fruit.

1997 SOAVE SUPERIORE
Fasoli Gino
Vinceremos, HDRA £4.99
Certified organic, vegan
Soave itself has a 'pile 'em high, sell 'em cheap' reputation, not helped by co-operatives churning out high volumes at low prices; but it *is* possible to find examples that actually taste of something. Try this: a rich, ripe, creamy nose, lots of soft ripe citrussy fruit and a decent finish. All this for (just) under a fiver.

SPAIN

1998 LA MANCHA
Mundo de Yuntero
Vintage Roots £3.90
Certified organic, vegetarian
Fresh, light nose, soft and fruity with good concentration of flavour for the price. And a very elegant blue bottle.

1998 XARELLO D'ANYADA, PENEDÈS
Albet i Noya
Vintage Roots £4.99
Certified organic, vegan
This had more to show on the nose than in the mouth, which was

rather a shame. Very fragrant on the nose, the fruit is fresh and
lively, and it's interesting to taste the Xarello grape on its own – it
usually disappears into anonymity in the blend of base wines for
Cava. Ultimately, though, the fruit, while showing good depth,
was too neutral.

GREECE

1998 MANTINIA ORINO
Domaine Spiropoulos
Vintage Roots £4.95; Vinceremos, HDRA £4.99
Certified organic, vegan
This is one of those wines where you need to look past the label –
in this case an incredibly naff purple stag at bay on a bed of pink
vine leaves. Hide it in a wine cooler, though, and you can enjoy a
very attractive, lively, fresh wine with good fruit. And as it's made
entirely from indigenous variety Moshofilero, you can confuse
wine buffs with it. It's great to see local varieties reach an
international audience. One to encourage.

WHITES OVER £5

FRANCE

1998 GRAND PREBOIS
Vin de Pays de la Principauté d'Orange
Perrin
Adnams £5.25
Certified organic
Another Perrin wine that belies its humble 'country wine' origin.

Stylish and elegant with peachy flavours and a long finish. Very good value and very well made.

1997 LA VIEILLE FERME
Côtes du Ventoux
Bibendum £5.28; Roberson £5.95 (also sometimes sighted in Tesco)
Converting to organic
This wine comes from the region made infamous by Peter Mayle's *A Year in Provence*, but don't let that put you off. It's hot down there, certainly, but the vineyards that produce this wine face north so the heat is less fierce, the grapes ripen that bit more slowly and the chance for complexity in the resulting wine is that much greater. The nose reminded me of beansprouts and hazelnuts, a heady combination, I'm sure you'll agree. The taste is refreshingly sharp and concentrated: lively ripe fruit, intense buttery flavour, a result of the mix of southern French varieties including Grenache and Roussanne. I've labelled this estate, part of the consistently good Perrin stable, 'converting to organic'; in fact they've practised organic methods for years, and are now in the process of getting the official certification.

1997/8 DOMAINE DE L'ECU
Muscadet de Sèvre et Maine Sur Lie
Guy Bossard
Vinceremos, HDRA, Organic Wine Company £5.29; Safeway £5.49
Certified organic, vegan
Guy Bossard is one of those guys whose commitment shines out through his wines. This man makes classic Muscadet 'sur lie' – smell the zingy yeastiness from all those months absorbing flavour from the lees. It's so fresh you almost think you can taste a salty tang borne in from the Atlantic. Farming organically since 1975, Bossard still works the land with horses, but in the winery he takes advantage of the most modern technology. Old vines – 45 to 50

years old – mean the juice from his grapes is more concentrated, and low yields improve the concentration further. You may be paying closer to £6 rather than the £4.50 the cheapest Muscadet costs, but you're buying a wine of sound provenance and top quality. Those rock-bottom Muscadets taint the whole region with a poor reputation. Try Bossard and discover what Muscadet can taste like in the hands of a committed organic expert.

1997 TOURAINE SAUVIGNON
Domaine de la Garrelière
Vinceremos, HDRA £5.29
Certified organic, vegan
Touraine, the less well-regarded central Loire area, seems to offer a potent source for expressive organic whites, and this is no exception. Bags of fruit with unexpected tropical notes, even the odd hint of mango. It's crisp and lively and very refreshing.

1998 TOURAINE SAUVIGNON
Domaine des Maisons Brulées
Vintage Roots £5.40
Certified organic, biodynamic, vegetarian
With this bone-dry wine you can enjoy refreshing acidity balanced by a good concentration of fruit – all those fresh gooseberry flavours, and fortunately no cats' pee in evidence. If you're a fan of Sauvignon Blanc this is a good example at a much more modest price than the grander Sancerre just down the road.

1998 CHARDONNAY
Vin de Pays de l'Aude
Domaine de Brau
Vintage Roots £5.75
Certified organic, vegan
More winning wine from organic stalwarts Domaine de Brau. Inviting gold colour, masses of soft ripe fruit perfectly balanced by oak. Real style and class and incredibly good value.

1996 PINOT BLANC
Domaine Eugène Meyer
Vinceremos, HDRA £6.49; T&W Wines £10.10
Biodynamic, certified organic, vegan

A family domaine making wine in Alsace for nearly 400 years that converted to biodynamics in 1969 and never looked back. They find it makes the vines 'more receptive to cosmic forces, creating harmony between the earth and the atmosphere'. Everything is certainly harmonious in this wine which offers a very clean, clear expression of Pinot Blanc, as you might expect from a biodynamic estate. Ripe, well rounded, with good acidity, this wine gives the lie to any idea that Pinot Blanc is a neutral, workhorse kind of grape. There's personality here. Pinot Blanc can produce terrific wines if the winemaker's good enough.

1998 COTEAUX D'AIX-EN-PROVENCE
Domaine Terres Blanches
Vintage Roots £6.99
Certified organic, biodynamic, vegan

Blended from the southern French varieties of Bourboulenc and Grenache Blanc, this wine offers unusual and interesting flavours – something to value in these days of increasingly standardised wines. Powerful aromas jump out of the glass – Provençal herbs, perhaps? – and in the mouth it's dry, a mix of ripe fruit flavours, lively and refreshing, nicely concentrated. This is well worth experimenting with if you're bored with the usual run-of-the-mill stuff.

1997 RIESLING
André Stentz
Organic Wine Company £7.29
Certified organic

A good example of my favourite white grape from Alsace where the style is generally fuller and rounder than in Germany. No shortage of acidity, though, to balance the fruit. Alsace wines, despite being nearly all white, have the attack and acidity to cut through the fattiness and heartiness of local cuisine, which makes them perfect food wines. If you're looking to play with exotic food-and-wine pairings, try this and see what works for you.

1998 SANCERRE
Christian and Nicole Dauny
Vintage Roots £7.50
Certified organic, vegan

Sancerre has a reputation for steeliness – elegance, austerity, not a wine to cuddle up with. Or to. If you like Sauvignon Blanc, this end of the Loire is the place to aspire to. A famous name like this doesn't come cheap, and many Sancerres are dilute, lank things not worthy of the name. This, on the other hand, with its clear structure and depth, has a lot to offer: a classic minerally nose, crisp, austere, very nervy and nuanced, and finely balanced.

1997 PETIT CHABLIS
Domaine Jean Goulley
Vintage Roots £7.95
Certified organic, vegan

Lively nose and decent lemony fruit from the only certified Chablis producer. A steely, crisp Burgundy from this northern outpost of the appellation.

1996 TOKAY-PINOT GRIS
Domaine Eugène Meyer
Vinceremos, HDRA £7.99
Certified organic, biodynamic, vegan

Pinot Gris is such a delicious grape, one of my all-time favourites, and I'm so pleased to learn its star is rising in Alsace: Pinot Gris now represents 10 per cent of grapes grown there. This may not have the sinuous smokiness of really first-class examples but it's good value; round and rich in the mouth, with a long finish, and good balancing acidity which means it works well with rich food.

1997 MÂCON-CLESSÉ
Domaine René Michel
Mayfair Cellars (020 7329 8899, case sales only); Tradition
£9.85, Oak-aged £10.75 (roughly)
Eco

I first visited this winery for my wine tourism guides, and they give good visit. Now in its sixth generation, the Michels farm this estate with infinite care and attention to detail, which even extends to the neatness of the fine gravel floor in their barrel cellar. The tiny stones are raked in elaborate patterns and all I could do was gaze respectfully at it from the safety of the entrance. Walking over it seemed sacrilegious. Here there are wines of fine quality, a clean expression of Chardonnay with leanness and elegance. Choose between unoaked (Tradition) and oaked styles.

1996 PESSAC-LÉOGNAN
Château Haut Nouchet
Vintage Roots £9.95
Certified organic, vegan

Very nice number, this – excellent concentration and depth of fruit, elegant, well structured, a very high-quality wine. Lots of ripe fruit for both nose and mouth, and oak, but kept well in balance. Pessac-Léognan lies within the Graves area of Bordeaux, and this is a fine example. Good dinner party choice.

1997 RIESLING WINTZENHEIM
Domaine Zind-Humbrecht
Wine Rack £10.49; Anthony Byrne Fine Wine £11.25
Eco, converting to biodynamic

A fine young Riesling – nervy, finely balanced, full of fresh fruit but with depth coming from rigorously low yields. I'd say this wine has a long path to travel – it won't be fully mature for several years yet, giving that rich oily style so beloved of Riesling aficionados (me too). Yet it's drinking so well now, it'll be hard to have the patience to sit back and let it develop.

1997 COUDOULET DE BEAUCASTEL BLANC
Côtes du Rhône
Perrin
Adnams £11.55, plus Oddbins, Tanners and others
Certified organic
A real blockbuster of a wine, with huge gobs of oak and
gooseberry and apricot fruit on the nose. Initially it promised more
than it delivered – the palate couldn't seem to follow through and
offer the equivalent power in taste, as it was overwhelmed by the
oak. I tried it again, later, with a plate of garlicky roasted
vegetables. The wine threw off its inhibitions, stepped out of the
trees and completely seduced me. Just goes to show what happens
when you taste a wine with its natural companion – good food –
rather than in isolation.

1996 MÂCON-CLESSÉ, QUINTAINE
Guillemot-Michel
T&W Wines £12.40
Certified organic, biodynamic
This really has got to be one of the most amazing white
Burgundies I have ever come across. Marc and Pierrette Guillemot
have shown consistent commitment to their production from the
moment they bought themselves out of membership of the local
co-operative (price: one year's harvest), preferring to produce a
small amount of high-quality wine rather than contribute to the
vast quantity of dilute, vapid stuff Mâcon is rightly infamous for.

The commitment of this young couple to making the best they
possibly can borders on the obsessive. At harvest, for example,
they taste their way right through the vineyard, sampling the
grapes still on the vine, and tagging any individual vines they feel
are doing something special – above-average flavour or
concentration. Then, in February, they'll come back and take
cuttings from these vines to create their ideal vineyard.

After three years in organic production they moved on to
biodynamics, which, if you taste this luscious wine, truly allows

the purest expression of Chardonnay to shine through. The grapes are hand harvested and only natural yeasts are used. They don't use oak, not even old barrels, preferring to allow the Chardonnay to speak for itself (which it does, very loudly). It offers a clarity and complexity rarely found in Mâcon wines, a richness and depth that makes you want to reach for the bottle again and again.

1997 ALSACE PINOT GRIS, HERRENWEG DE TURCKHEIM
Domaine Zind-Humbrecht
Threshers, Bottoms Up £12.99
Eco, converting to biodynamic

Olivier Humbrecht makes some of the finest wines in Alsace, competing with top winemakers all over the world. His recent decision to convert his vineyards to biodynamics is yet more proof of the sheer effectiveness of this method: as he put it, he converted 'to ensure keeping our soils and vineyards in good condition and alive for the future'.

His wines are characterised by a fullness and richness that are a world away from the thin, acidic Alsace wines some of the co-operatives produce. This Pinot Gris is a delight: rich, spicy, smoky, a wonderful multi-dimensional wine. Zind-Humbrecht really is one of those names you can buy with confidence throughout his extensive range.

1991 GEWURZTRAMINER GRAND CRU SPIEGEL
Domaine Eugène Meyer
T&W Wines £16.39
Certified organic, biodynamic, vegan

If you like Gewurztraminer – and, let's be fair, it isn't to everyone's taste, with its blowsy, cabbage-rose and lychees perfumes – then this is one of the finest examples you'll find. It's fat and ripe and almost overpowering. The biodynamic methods which extract such a pure, clean essence of grape and soil, coupled with the Grand Cru site – one of the best vineyards in Alsace – add up to a very heady mix. Approach slowly, drink with reverence.

1997 GEWURZTRAMINER ALTENBOURG, CUVÉE LAURENCE
Domaine Weinbach
Justerini & Brooks (020 7493 8721) £28.00
Eco
Colette Faller and her daughters have been producing wines of
extraordinary concentration and fullness from the walled Clos des
Capucins vineyards outside Kaysersberg in Alsace for long enough
to have acquired an outstanding reputation. Their house style is
for full, rich, lush wines, none more so than this golden Gewurz,
all heady perfumes and oily, unctuous fruit, and a finish to last
forever. A wine to drink on its own, slowly.

ITALY

1998 VERDICCHIO DEI CASTELLI DI JESI CLASSICO
Moncaro
Waitrose £4.79
Certified organic
Verdicchio's the grape, grown in Italy since at least the fourteenth
century. The name derives from the greenish-yellow tinge to the
grape skin. Plenty of lemony acidity, and a characteristic bitter-
almond aftertaste, mark Moncaro's wine out as one of the best
examples of this classic Italian white. Once again, organically
produced grapes deliver freshness, clarity and all the prime
characteristics of the variety.

1998 PINOT GRIGIO
Perlage
Vinceremos, HDRA £5.29
Certified organic, vegan
A very user-friendly wine. In Italy, Pinot Gris becomes Pinot
Grigio and often loses something in the translation – maybe you
won't find all that unctuous, rich multi-layered smoky fruit so
readily here. At this price, let's face it, it's unlikely; but you will

find some heady aromatic wafts on the nose, and lots of summer fruit to taste.

1998 SOAVE SUPERIORE
Fasoli Gino
Vintage Roots £5.35
Certified organic, vegan
Soave can be bland and dull. Not this one. Here you have fab concentration of fruit giving you intense flavours: it's crisp, refreshing, with juicy acidity and a long finish (always a good sign). A really good example.

GERMANY

1997 DEIDESHEIMER HERRGOTTSACKER
Riesling Kabinett Trocken
Reichsrat von Buhl
T&W Wines £10.39
German wine labels . . . doncha just love 'em? About as penetrable as the Finnish for 'organic' ('luonnomukainen', since you ask).

So, let's take it from the top. First line is the place, Deidesheim ('-er' means 'from', as in Hamburger). Herrgottsacker is the name of the vineyard. Often these names translate rather sweetly. This one means 'the Lord God's acre'. (My favourite, incidentally, is Bernkasteler Badstube, Bernkastel bathroom. What *did* they do there?)

At the bottom we have the producer's name. Looks like the estate's founding father was an imperial counsellor.

Sandwiched in the middle is the grape variety, the blessed Riesling, then Kabinett, the lowest, most light and fragrant rung on the German special quality wine ladder. 'Trocken' on a German wine label isn't always such good news. It means 'dry', which isn't a problem in itself, but German wines by nature tend to have some residual sweetness. Indeed, it's prized; but a few years ago there was a fashion in Germany for making dry wines, the better to accompany food. The result, in all too many cases, was hollow wine, with biting acidity and no sweet fruit to counteract it.

Here, of course, it's different. This is God's acre, after all. It's light and fresh, in classic Kabinett style, and the acidity is properly balanced with clear, light Riesling flavours. It's actually surprisingly complex. Yes, you're right. I liked it.

AUSTRIA

1997 GRINZINGER REISENBURG
Franz Mayer
Vintage Roots £5.45
Certified organic, vegan
Although Austria's pretty hot on organic wine production it finds few friends among wine consumers. This wine proves that's a shame. It's an interesting blend of six grape varieties including Riesling, Pinot Blanc and Grüner Veltliner. The six varieties don't slug it out for your attention, either; it's a harmonious blend with excellent concentration and depth of fruit, plus a good backbone of acidity and a decent finish.

SPAIN

1998/9 RIOJA GENOLI
Viña Ijalba
Vintage Roots £5.99
Converting to organic
A very, very fresh, fragrant nose and huge, fresh, mouthfilling fruit. There's a hint of sweetness here and good concentration, but it's still sufficiently lightweight to enjoy alone, without food.

1997 MACABEU COL.LECCIO, PENEDÈS
Albet i Noya
Vintage Roots £9.45
Almost New World in its exotic tropical-fruit aromas and liberal
addition of oak. Deep gold in colour, very full, ripe and rewarding.

GREECE

1996 THALASSITIS
Gaia Winery
Oddbins £6.99
Eco
I ought to tell you, first of all, that this winery purifies the water
used for the bottling line and general winery operations by keeping
eels in the rainwater tanks . . . The wine is made on Santorini
island where organic principles tend to be widely practised, blessed
as it is with a hot dry climate and volcanic soils. The Assyrtiko
grapes are a variety indigenous to Greece, and it's good that the
new wave of winemaking out there is alive to the possibilities of
home-grown varieties rather than slavishly copying 'international'
styles. It's bone dry: perfect with shellfish.

UNITED STATES

1996 CHARDONNAY
Fetzer Bonterra
*Waitrose, Tesco, Oddbins, Wine Cellar, Sainsbury's, Fuller's
£7.99; Rackhams £8.75; Organic Wine Company £8.79;
Vinceremos, HDRA £8.99; Vintage Roots £9.50*
Certified organic
All barrel-fermented for extra elegance, this has a citrus, buttery
nose, and is full and rich on the palate. Great balance, crisp, in
more of a Burgundy style with pronounced but balanced oak.

1997 VOIGNIER
Fetzer Bonterra
Fuller's £9.99
Certified organic
Dear for a non-Condrieu Voignier, and heavier-bodied than some, but interesting nonetheless – peaches, violets on the nose and a delicious long finish. Try this with crab, for instance, for a delicious contrast with the sweet white meat.

1998 SAUVIGNON BLANC, NAPA VALLEY
Frog's Leap
Morris & Verdin £11.50; Lay & Wheeler (01206 560002) £12.75
Mostly certified organic, converting to biodynamic
I should explain that the 'mostly' means that the four vineyards of this estate are certified. Frog's Leap also buys in grapes from other growers who farm organically, of which four are certified and three aren't.

This Sauvignon is enticing and creamy (thanks to the addition of 4 per cent of Semillon) with an immense depth of flavour. The acidity is admirably balanced, the fruit is rich and lingers on long after you've swallowed the last drop.

1998 CHARDONNAY, CARNEROS
Frog's Leap
Lay & Wheeler £16.50; Morris & Verdin £17.00
Mostly certified organic, converting to biodynamic
Simply gorgeous. Honeyed, creamy fruit, yet lean and light, everything perfectly balanced and integrated. A great advertisement for the success of organic and biodynamic cultivation in bringing vineyards back from the dead.

AUSTRALIA

1998 CHENIN/CHARDONNAY/SAUVIGNON, VICTORIA
Robinvale Vineyard
Vintage Roots £6.99
Certified biodynamic, vegan
Great depth of flavour here, good acidity, and a long, long finish.
The three varieties together are a bit like cats in a sack, varietal
character muddied as they slug it out, but it packs a punch.

1997 CHARDONNAY
Robinvale Vineyard
Vintage Roots £7.40
Certified organic, biodynamic
Assailed at once by powerful oak on the nose, the faint of heart
might quail: not another OTT Aussie Chardonnay? But no. This
wine was barrel-fermented, so it came into contact with oak from
day one; and that kind of contact lends elegance and finesse to a
wine, maybe makes it more Burdundian in style. It's rich,
concentrated, intense, and the taste of oak is indeed assertive; but
it's not blowsy or overblown. Rather good, actually.

1997 PENFOLDS CLARE VALLEY CHARDONNAY/SAUVIGNON BLANC
EH Booth, Waitrose, Selfridges, Anthony Byrne Fine Wines,
Classic Wines £7.99
Certified organic, vegan
Penfolds is the only major winemaker in Australia to have grasped
the nettle of organic production. They began converting part of
their Clare Valley estate in 1991 and produced its first fully
organic vintage in 1994.

Aspersions have been cast on the organic-ness of Clare Valley
wines, so I checked with their technical manager, who came back
with the following assurance: 'The vineyard in which the grapes
for Penfolds' organic wines are grown and the winery in which the

wines are made are certified by the National Association for
Sustainable Agriculture, Australia (NASAA). The grapes are grown
and the wines are made in accordance with NASAA guidelines for
organic products. NASAA is accredited by IFOAM (International
Federation of Organic Agriculture Movements) and recognised by
AQIS (Australian Quarantine Inspection Service), the Australian
competent authority.'

Short of being in the vineyard and winery from start to finish,
we have to accept that this official monitoring ensures that the
wine is what it claims to be.

This wine is one-third Sauvignon to two-thirds Chardonnay, and
you'll notice the Chardonnay predominating, but unlike some
blends the two varieties do make up a harmonious whole. The wine
was fermented in new and newish barrels rather than vats, which
always lends a wine an extra touch of finesse – and oak, of course.
(You can certainly taste the oak but it doesn't shout its presence, for
which I was grateful.) Once fermented the wine sits on its lees for
three months. This technique was pioneered in Muscadet in the
Loire valley, where it gives a fresh, yeasty zip to an otherwise rather
neutral wine. Here it also adds a dimension of yeasty zing to a
complex, well-structured wine. I'm not always a fan of
Chardonnay/Sauvignon Blanc blends, but this works really well.

When this sells out there'll be a bit of a wait for the new vintage
because they didn't make a 1998 and the 1999 won't hit the
shelves until late summer 2000. Grab the '97 while you can.

1995 RIESLING, ADELAIDE HILLS
Glenara Vineyard
Vinceromos, HDRA £7.99; Vintage Roots £8.95
Certified organic, vegan
I have to be honest, I'm not usually a great fan of Aussie Riesling. I
think it's a grape that gives of its best in a marginal, cool climate,
and in the heat of Australia it can all too easily lose its finesse and
the elegance so many people call 'racy'. Well, this is different. On
the nose it gives you that characteristic oily, petrolly bouquet of

fine German or Alsatian Riesling, and it follows through on the palate with intense citrussy fruit, but with added richness from the warmer climate. Well-balanced acidity and a long finish round things off very nicely, thank you. Something of a revelation, really.

1997 SAUVIGNON BLANC
Eden Ridge
Vinceremos, HDRA £8.99
Eco, vegetarian
Based near Adelaide, this estate has Provence-like weather which makes it ideal for organic production. Eden Ridge prices have risen steeply over the past two years, and I don't think it's justified on the basis of what I tasted here. The wine is refreshing but very full on the palate and doesn't actually taste much like Sauvignon to my mind.

NEW ZEALAND

1997 SEMILLON/CHARDONNAY
Millton Vineyard
Vinceremos, HDRA £5.49
Certified organic, biodynamic, vegan
From one of New Zealand's finest winemakers comes this full, ripe, rich blend. Crisp and aromatic, the fruit fills the mouth but isn't over the top; no hitting you over the head with blowsy lychees and pineapples here, and the wine's all the better for it. James Millton aims to make wines 'giving an expression of the natural flavours found in the grapes harvested from our vineyards in the Gisborne region. I wish as well to enhance the life quality of the land we are responsible for and in doing so leave it in an improved state for future generations.'

1996 CHARDONNAY
Richmond Plains
Vinceremos, HDRA £6.79
Certified organic, vegan
This was the first estate to be certified organic in the South Island
of New Zealand (James Millton, the first overall, is on North
Island) from plantings begun in 1991. So the vines are still pretty
juvenile but already showing well, as in this Chardonnay which
offers marmaladey fruit – not an obvious Chardonnay
characteristic, I grant you – and assertive wood.

1996 BARREL-FERMENTED CHENIN BLANC
Millton Vineyard
Vinceremos, HDRA £6.99
Eco, biodynamic, vegan
Bags of zesty fruit, ripe and rich and very clearly Chenin. Highly
recommended. This wine is listed as eco rather than certified
organic because of James Millton's problems with mealy bug
infestation in 1994 (see pages 22–23).

1996 BARREL-FERMENTED CHARDONNAY
Millton Vineyard
Vinceremos, HDRA £8.49
Eco, biodynamic
Wonderful stuff – delicious creamy fruit, with the nose and taste of
vanilla and butter. Fermenting in barrel makes the wine more
expensive (barrels cost over £100 a throw) but lends structure,
class, elegance ... it's only not certified organic because of, again,
the mealy bug affair (see above).

1998 RESERVE CHARDONNAY
Cromwell, Central Otago
Kawarau Estate
Vintage Roots £11.99
Certified organic, vegan
A remarkable wine. At 14.5 per cent alcohol it's not for the

fainthearted or indeed the driver. Take a heady aroma of all things tropical, add a large dose of oak, light the blue touch paper and stand back five yards. The flavours explode on the palate and spin round like a catherine wheel. Unfortunately the wine is in short supply so grab it while you can.

SOUTH AFRICA

1998 CAP SOLEIL CHARDONNAY
Sonop Wine Farm
Vintage Roots £5.50
Certified organic, vegan
Made by the only certified organic estate in South Africa, this is a very good example of ripe buttery Chardonnay flavour. Stick your nose in this for great depth of fruit and bags of flavour. A really honest expression of the fruit in the best organic tradition: nothing overblown about it in that sometimes rather overemphatic Aussie style. Vintage Roots say it's a big seller, and I'm not surprised. Look out also for their Sauvignon Blanc.

REDS UNDER £5

FRANCE

SAFEWAY ORGANIC RED
Vin de Pays du Gard
Jacques Frelin
Safeway £3.69
Certified organic, vegan
Jacques Frelin has carved out a difficult life path for himself – he is an organic négociant, both making his own wines and working

with other growers, buying their grapes or wines they have made.
So not only does he have to keep track of his own organic
production, he also has to make sure all his suppliers adhere to
organic regulations throughout the process. Not easy.

This wine is of his own production; a light, fresh nose smelling
of red fruits – cherry, strawberry – a well-balanced, light body,
and tasting slightly spicy, with an underlying earthy, rustic
character. Serve anywhere, anytime, with food or on its own – this
wine doesn't stand on ceremony.

1997 FRENCH ORGANIC RED
Vin de Pays de l'Hérault
Domaine de Savignac
Vinceremos, HDRA £3.89
Certified organic, vegan
It's that man again – Jacques Frelin. This is his second estate (busy
man) in deepest southern France, and it offers workmanlike,
decent drinking with no uncouth hard tannins to get in your way.
Very fair for the price.

1997 ORGANIC ROUGE
Vin de Pays des Côtes de Thongue
Louis Delhon
Vintage Roots £3.90
Certified organic, vegan
Fresh and clean, with plenty of ripe fruit, this is an honest bottle and
a great house red. It's made by a stalwart of the Vintage Roots list,
Domaine Bassac near Beziers. (Louis Dehlon is their winemaker.)

1998 VIN DE PAYS DE L'AUDE
Domaine de Brau
Vintage Roots £4.10
Certified organic, vegan
A wine of considerable youth that would have benefited from a
little longer in bottle (and by the time you read this it'll probably

have had just that). This is rustic and approachable – and its price makes it very popular.

1996 MERLOT LE MAGICIEN
Vin de Pays des Monts de la Grage
Vinceremos, HDRA £4.29
Certified organic, vegetarian
What a disappointment. I thought there was a naked man on the wine label but closer inspection reveals he's wearing a bodysuit. Oh well. And the wine? Thick and unctuous, well-balanced, slightly sweet fruit. Quite a bargain, really.

1998 VIN DE PAYS D'OC, MERLOT
Domaine de Picheral
Vinceremos, HDRA £4.49
Certified organic, vegan
A vegetal nose, all stalky, like old cabbage leaves (what an appetising occupation this is). The tannins are quite firm, with some hard edges, but there's good fruit to back it up, and a rather attractive smokiness on the finish.

1998 CABARDÈS
Jacques Frelin
Vinceremos, HDRA £4.49
Certified organic, vegan
Cabardès, tucked away near Carcassonne in the Midi, blends Cabernet and Merlot – very unusual in these parts. Full of deep chocolatey flavours, the wine is rich and dark with rustic tannins and masses of jammy ripe fruit. A wine with elbows – i.e. it packs a terrific punch – and a lot of character for under a fiver.

1998 ST-CHINIAN
Domaine des Soulié
Vinceremos, HDRA £4.49
Certified organic, vegan

The clear whiff of blackberries on the nose and pungent flavours of Rhône-style reds spring from the blend of Carignan, Grenache and Syrah. St-Chinian is north of Beziers, so it's part of the Mediterranean sprawl of the Midi; but there's nothing of the wine lake about this. It would make an elegant partner to robust meaty food, but is probably best not drunk on its own.

1998 CABARDÈS
Château de Brau
Vintage Roots £4.50
Certified organic, vegan
The Atlantic meets the Mediterranean in a blend of Cabernet Sauvignon and Merlot with Grenache and Syrah. The result is a dry, earthy wine with ripe fruit and excellent structure.

1998 VIN DE PAYS DES COTEAUX DE MURVIEL, MERLOT
Domaine Bassac
Vintage Roots £4.50
Certified organic, vegetarian
Rustic, with plenty of ripe, brambly fruit, this is soft and easy to drink. Pity it's from yet another obscure vin de pays area, though that doesn't obscure the good value. Pass the atlas.

1998 COSTIÈRES DE NÎMES
Domaine Cabanis
Vinceremos, HDRA £4.59
Certified organic, vegetarian
This is such an attractive wine. The soft spicy blend of Carignan, Grenache and Mourvèdre welcomes you with open arms. The estate has farmed organically since 1984, and this wealth of experience, coupled with ageing in big oak casks, gives deeply flavoured fruit with no hard tannins getting in the way. Very good value.

1997 COTEAUX DU LANGUEDOC
Domaine la Fon de Lacan
Organic Wine Company £4.79
In second year of conversion to organic
A strong Syrah content to this robust country red, blended with
Grenache and Mourvèdre, gives a lively, reasonable value, easy-
drinking red. Yields are low so there's plenty of fruit in the glass.

1997 CÔTES DU RHÔNE
Cave la Vigneronne Villedieu
Vinceremos, HDRA £4.79
Certified organic, vegetarian
I thought this an excellent example of generic Côtes du Rhône:
rustic, good extract, deep brambly fruit, and a long finish. This
comes from a small co-operative in the southern Rhône – imagine
the co-ordination necessary to get every grower member to agree
to farm organically. Since co-operatives produce so much of
Europe's wine, co-operative co-operation is essential if we're to get
organic wines on our shelves in the kinds of quantities demanded.

1997 CÔTES DU RHÔNE
Vignoble de la Jasse
Vinceremos, HDRA £4.99
Certified organic, vegan
Here's another Côtes du Rhône, but in a completely contrasting
style. It's much lighter-bodied, a pale red, but again offering good
concentration: softer tannins than the Villedieu example, rounded
and spicy.

1997 CÔTES DU RHÔNE
Jacques Frelin
Vinceremos, HDRA £4.99
Certified organic
Pale red again, and light in style – rustic tannins and sparkling
jammy fruit. Some elegance here.

1996 CORBIÈRES
Château Pech-Latt
Waitrose £4.99
Certified organic

This wine just squeezes into the under-£5 category, and were it a pound or so cheaper I'd be a lot happier. I've read some rave reviews for this wine, which made it doubly disappointing that this bottle didn't measure up to them. I want vibrant fruit in an organic wine, a sense of life and vitality, and that simply wasn't there. Maybe there was just some variation between bottles and I was unlucky – it can happen.

ITALY

1998 SOLATIO ROSSO
Perlage
Vinceremos, HDRA £3.99
Certified organic, vegan

This blends top Italian varieties Sangiovese and Montepulciano with local grapes, and the result is a soft, light, approachable wine at a very fair price. No hard tannins here, but juicy acidity and pleasant, ripe plummy fruit. One of those reds to try on people who say they don't like red.

1998 MERLOT
Perlage
Vinceremos, HDRA £4.19
Certified organic, vegan

A lightish body and velvety cherry fruit, soft tannins and a reasonably soft price add up to very easy drinking. Not a winter warmer, maybe, but a good summer red, perfectly happy on its own.

1997 BARDOLINO CLASSICO
Ottomarzo
Vinceremos, HDRA £4.99
Certified organic, vegan

A very light red, this, full of light sweet fruit yet firm and creamy on the palate. Again, try this one on someone who insists they don't like red wine.

SPAIN

1998 LA MANCHA
Caballero de Mesarrubias
Vintage Roots £4.70
Certified organic, vegan

One that took me by surprise. Powerful and full flavoured, it has hidden depths of complexity that develop in the glass. All this for £4.70 . . .

1998 CAN VENDRELL TINTO, PENEDÈS
Albet i Noya
Vintage Roots £4.80; Vinceremos, HDRA £4.99
Certified organic, vegan

Oh yes, this is easy drinking. A very attractive red fruit nose, and they extract bags of ripe, juicy flavour from the Tempranillo grape by using the Beaujolais winemaking technique, carbonic maceration. The Albet i Noya family was one of the pioneers of organic viticulture in Spain, and clearly has plenty of expertise.

RED OVER £5

FRANCE

1998 CHÂTEAU DU GRAND PREBOIS
Côtes du Rhône
Perrin
Adnams £5.25
Certified organic
When there's so much indifferent Côtes du Rhône swilling around it's a pleasure to find one with as much character as this. It's dark and smoky with a whiff of hillside herbs. Truly a snip at the price.

1998 BIODYNAMIC ROUGE
Fiefs Vendeens
Vintage Roots £5.25
Certified organic, biodynamic, vegan
A companion bottle to the Biodynamic Blanc (see p. 129), with an equally assertive label, this wine is vivid purple with a faint smell of fried bread on the nose. Soft, ripe berry fruit flavours to follow, chewy and lively.

1997 LA VIEILLE FERME
Côtes du Ventoux
Bibendum £5.28 (and sometimes Tesco); Roberson £5.95
Converting to organic
The Perrin brothers, who produce the exceptional Château de Beaucastel wines, also run La Vieille Ferme, and the attention to detail so in evidence in the Beaucastel wines rubs off on this estate too. A deep purply red colour and with a meaty nose, you'll find lots of round, brambly fruit on the palate and rustic, softening tannins. And a finish that stays and stays with you.

1996 VIN DE PAYS DES COTEAUX DE CABRERISSE
Domaine de la Bouletière
Vinceremos, HDRA £5.29
Certified organic, vegetarian

I do wish they wouldn't do this – French winemakers seem to take
a perverse delight in creating ever-smaller and more obscure vin de
pays areas. How can we keep up and actually know where these
wines come from? I doubt anyone's actually named one after their
back garden yet, but it can only be a matter of time. So who
knows where Cabrerisse is? Somewhere in Corbières, I think. Not
that it matters – this wine is made by the Château de Caraguilhes,
who have carved out a considerable reputation for their organic
wine. This one blends Merlot with Carignan and Alicante (no, not
a tomato, not here) to make an attractively clean, light, medium-
bodied wine full of ripe fruit – an ideal barbecue companion.

1997 LA CIBOISE
Coteaux du Tricastin
Chapoutier
Unwins, Fuller's £5.39
Eco

Very seductive, oozes with ripe strawberry fruit. Soft, supple, and
altogether extremely drinkable.

1998 CABARDÈS CUVÉE EXQUISE
Château de Brau
Vintage Roots £5.49
Certified organic, vegan

A very attractive nose, inky dark with aromas of tobacco and
chocolate. It's a blend of the Bordeaux varieties Merlot and
Cabernet Sauvignon with the southern Grenache and Syrah, and
the result, after nine months in wood, is very attractive indeed –
and at this price, a bargain.

1996 VIN DE PAYS DE L'AUDE
Domaine Anthea
La Reserve £5.50
Certified organic, biodynamic
Sixties wild child Serge Ziggiotti makes wine with conviction and
zest; a lively, ripe nose, all strawberries and raspberries and
cherries and even a hint of mango. But despite all this spicy,
powerful fruit the wine still manages to be well balanced and
attractively integrated, no mean feat for just over a fiver.

1996/8 VALRÉAS
Domaine de la Grande Bellane
Vinceremos, HDRA £5.69
Certified organic
Valréas is a named village within the greater Côtes du Rhône lake,
villages that are singled out for special attention by virtue of
superior quality – in theory, anyway. And in practice too, in this
case. Grand Bellane manages to juggle both quality and quantity.
It makes wine in sufficient volume to supply supermarkets as well
as specialists, and the 1996 vintage also sufficiently impressed
dozens of judges to win Red Wine of the Year at the 1997
International Wine Challenge. This was the only French wine ever
to win a Wine of the Year award in any category, never mind an
organic wine. Here you'll find light, fresh sweet fruit, well put
together – enjoyable and reliable. The 1998 is also now on the
shelves, and it too is full of finely balanced ripe sweet fruit.
Luscious.

1996 ST-CHINIAN
Château Bousquette
Vinceremos, HDRA £5.69
Certified organic
Deeply coloured with a whiff of iodine on the nose, this southern
wine from deepest Languedoc has good grip, lots of concentrated
fruit and is an all-round good egg with food. Except eggs, of

course – not a good food to match with wine. Have you tasted that Burgundian dish *oeufs en meurette*, eggs poached in red wine? I rest my case.

1996 CORBIÈRES
Domaine Montmija
Roberson £5.95
Converting to organic

Corbières, another of the deep south French reds, can be inky dark and very tannic. Not this one, though – it's lighter than you might expect, made in a more modern style. A meaty nose gives way to a delightful creamy red-fruit mouthful. The tannins are mellow, the wine's well structured and the finish takes a while to finish. A really good deal for the price.

1995 MAS DE LA DAME
Les Baux de Provence
Allez Vins (01926 811969) £5.99
Eco

The estate of Mas de la Dame was immortalised on canvas by Van Gogh in 1889 and the vibrant colours of the painting somehow seem to insinuate themselves into the glass. This ripe southern French red simply oozes deep dark flavours, all chocolate and tobacco and earthy fruit.

1997 SAUMUR-CHAMPIGNY
Domaine des Frogères
Vinceremos, HDRA £5.99; Vintage Roots £6.50
Certified organic, vegan

Odd wine, this. I tasted it at both Vinceremos and Vintage Roots, and each time I thought there was something wrong with it. I kept thinking it was corky – you know, those strange, dusty, dull, 'off' flavours that mask what a wine really tastes like, like an overlay of clingfilm. I think in truth it's the house style, and it isn't going to be to everyone's taste. I usually like Saumur-Champigny, that lively, gutsy red made in Saumur from Cabernet Franc. It usually has bags of flavour and character. This has character too, in its own way. If you feel adventurous, see what you think.

1995 CHÂTEAU DE PRADE
Côtes de Castillon
GAEC Fournier et Fils
Co-op £5.99; Vintage Roots £6.25
Certified organic, vegetarian

This was the first organic wine the Co-op stocked, eight years ago, and it's stood the test of time (though not, of course, the same vintage). It's unusual to find an organic wine in this price bracket with some bottle age in these days of snap-'em-up young, so that makes this wine all the more interesting. Castillon lies in the less fashionable east end of Bordeaux; as so often, the under-regarded areas offer better value for money. It majors on Merlot, giving a ripe, round, meaty softness with lots of juicy fruit.

1996 MÂCON SUPÉRIEUR
Domaine de la Mollepierre
Allez Vins (01926 811969) £6.25
Certified organic

In Mâcon, as elsewhere in France, they have a very particular meaning for 'supérieur': an extra degree or half of alcohol. Nothing superior about it in terms of guaranteed better quality – that's something we have to judge for ourselves. And here, I do believe we've found it.

This is a red Mâcon, from the Gamay grape that produces the vibrant fruity Beaujolais wines just a few miles further south. There's none of the green steeliness of many Mâcon Gamays here. Instead the fruit is well rounded and ripe, with good balance and acidity and very refreshing. One of those reds to pour for people who claim not to like red.

1998 RÉGNIÉ
Christian Ducroix
Vintage Roots £6.45
Certified biodynamic, vegan

Beaujolais has ten 'crus' or growths, each named after a village deemed to produce wine of class and typicality, offering the best of the region. Régnié was the most recent to achieve this honour, in 1998, and there are those that reckon it doesn't merit this distinction. Not on this showing, however. This wine bursts with fruit on the nose, and offers classic Beaujolais style – ripe cherry fruit with good depth.

1997 VACQUEYRAS
Domaine le Clos de Caveau
Vinceremos, HDRA £6.49
Certified organic, vegetarian

Medium-bodied, with ripe sweet fruit, this southern Rhône wine betrays its origins in the spicy pepperiness of the blend of Grenache, Syrah, Mourvèdre and Cinsault. It really is drinking well: mouthfilling, lean and lively.

1996 CÔTES DU RHÔNE, CUVÉE PRESTIGE
Domaine St-Apollinaire
Vintage Roots £6.75
Certified biodynamic, vegan

One hundred per cent Syrah, from the heart of the spicy Rhône. Here we have medium body, juicy fruit and a long finish – but not too heavy. Good choice for Syrah fans and a good introduction if you're new to this luscious grape. Any sulphur-sensitives should home in on this one, as it claims no sulphur content.

1996 COMTE CATHARE
Roberson £6.95
Certified biodynamic

Robert Eden, the English winemaker at Comte Cathare, first
decided there was something in biodynamics while keeping bees:
he observed how everything the bees did was in harmony with the
seasons and the planets. The name refers back to the ancient
Cathar legends of the fabled knights guarding their ancient
knowledge in the south of France. The wine is lean, refined and
subtle, with well-concentrated ripe fruit and soft tannins.
Apparently this wine is popular with a younger age group. Yoof
wine? Surely not.

1997 CÔTES DE PROVENCE
Domaine Richeaume, Cuvée Tradition
Henning Hoesch
Vinceremos, HDRA £6.99; Yapp (01747 860423) £7.25
Certified organic, vegan

Spectacular wine made in a spectacular setting. A blend of
Cabernet Sauvignon and the usual Provençal suspects. It has a
richness and depth that reflects the passion of winemaker Henning
Hoesch. You might want to order a case – one bottle will probably
not seem quite enough. Wonderful stuff.

1996 CORBIÈRES, CUVÉE FUTS DE CHENE
Château de Lastours
*Booths of Stockport £7.20, plus various small independent
merchants*
Certified organic

Château de Lastours is an admirable institution. It's run as an
'occupational rehabilitation centre' which supports 60 people with
learning difficulties who work with staff to tend the vines and
make the wines. It also powers itself from a wind farm, the largest
in Europe. A few years ago their wines were in major multiples,
but now stockists have shrunk. Why? On the evidence of the wine

I tasted, it's a matter of overpricing. The wine simply doesn't offer the quality its rivals do at the price. That's a real shame.

1995 ST-ÉMILION
Château Pouchaud-Larquey
Vinceremos, HDRA £7.49
Certified organic, vegetarian
From my favourite part of Bordeaux, if I have such a thing, comes this rather fine example of Merlot-based wine. A vinous, sinuous nose, medium-bodied and quite rich, with a bitter chocolate finish. Good complexity for the price.

1996 ST-CHINIAN, COMTE CATHARE
Château de Combebelle
Vintage Roots £7.50
Certified biodynamic, vegan
A southern French wine claiming Cathar connections, this has soft tannins (not always something you can take for granted from down here) and lots of ripe red fruit to smell and taste. You know – blackberry, cherry – after all, when did a wine ever taste like wine?

1997 BOURGOGNE CÔTE CHALONNAISE
D'Heilly-Huberdeau
Vintage Roots £7.70
Certified organic, vegetarian
Another less fashionable area, the Côte Chalonnaise lies to the south of Burgundy and, while the wines don't have the sheer elegance of the golden slopes further north, they do have a luscious rustic charm. This is a fantastic example – raspberry, cherry fruit, light and elegant, and well structured but not too sweet. Vintage Roots say it sells consistently well, which is hardly surprising – the price is fair for the quality.

1996 CÔTES DE PROVENCE
Domaine des Fouques
T&W Wines £7.99
Biodynamic

A really satisfactory price–quality rapport here. The golden palm tree on the label sets the scene for some lush southern fruit – Syrah and Grenache – and a juicy wine of depth which is voluptuous, sensuous and an absolute steal at the price. Just mind how you pronounce it.

1995 CÔTES DE BOURG
Château Falfas
Vintage Roots £7.99
Certified organic, biodynamic

A truly extraordinary wine. From its delightful ruby red colour to the finely nuanced, subtle feel of the wine in the mouth, and a finish that goes on forever, this is biodynamics at its best. If the rest of Bordeaux would follow Falfas' lead, their wines might be worth drinking again.

1995 ST-CHINIAN
Château de Combebelle
Roberson £8.75
Converting to organic

Nothing posh or pretentious about this wine – a slightly rustic style, honest and down-to-earth, lots of well-integrated fruit and tannin and wonderful chocolatey aromas. Like the Green and Brown organic dark chocolate, rich and smoky.

1998 RASTEAU
Domaine du Trapadis
Gauntley's of Nottingham (0115 911 0555) £8.85
Eco

Rasteau, a prominent village in the southern Côtes du Rhône, produces hot, heady, rustic reds, and Domaine du Trapadis is up there with the hottest – bags of rich, ripe fruit and a leanness and balance you don't always find here. No filtration either, so you'll find a welcome deposit at the bottom of the bottle.

1996 MORGON
Gérard Bedlaïd
Roberson £9.50
Certified organic
Morgon is another of the 'crus' of Beaujolais: one of ten villages deemed to make the best wines in the region and allowed to distinguish themselves by putting the village name on the label. This one's very approachable, with lots of elegant fruit. Beaujolais is the perfect red wine to pour for people who say they don't like red wine, because it's soft and fruity with no hard tannins, so if there's someone you'd like to seduce into becoming a red wine drinker, try them on this.

1997 BOURGOGNE PINOT NOIR
Heresztyn
The Winery £9.50
Eco
The father grew onions in Gevrey-Chambertin. Now the son makes wine, good wine, but he finds having a Polish name doesn't make things easy in Burgundy. This wine, however, is easy on the eye – a delightful light cherry red – and on the palate. The tannins are softening, allowing the fruit from these young Gevrey-Chambertin vines to peep through. Classic Pinot Noir, despite the lowly appellation.

1996 LES BAUX-DE-PROVENCE
Château Romanin
Vintage Roots £9.75
Certified biodynamic, vegan
Les Baux-de-Provence gave the world bauxite and has an odd lunar-like landscape, all dramatic jagged rock. It's one of southern

France's tourist traps, full of wildly expensive starred hotel-restaurants and other tourist-fleecing operations. The wine from the region is similarly variable, but at its best it offers that rich, plummy, baked fruit the south of France can be so good at. This here's a good example: lean and restrained, with multi-layered juicy fruit and good structure from the Grenache/Syrah/Mourvèdre/Cabernet blend. Buy this if you want to wear your heart on your sleeve, because the label does: to point up its biodynamic origins it features the sun, the moon and a star.

1996 DOMAINE DES BEATES
Coteaux d'Aix-en-Provence
Chapoutier
Michael Morgan, Gauntley's of Nottingham £9.99
Eco
It would be very unfair to call this wine a lesser version of the Terra d'Or (see p. 168). It stands by itself as a rich, earthy red with bags of flavour and softening tannins. Aix-en-Provence seems to be a fertile source of powerful organic reds – certainly an area to watch.

1995 COTEAUX D'AIX-EN-PROVENCE, CUVÉE AURELIA
Domaine des Terres Blanches
Vinceremos, HDRA £9.99
Certified organic, vegetarian
Inky-purple baked ripe fruit, very rich and spicy but bone dry and with good acidity. Winemaker Noel Michelin won the Organic Wine Challenge in the days when it was still held (watch out for a revival, you can be sure someone's on to it already). If you're even a teeny bit fanciful you can imagine you smell the heady scents of the garrigue.

1998 MONTIRIUS VACQUEYRAS
Eric and Christine Saurel
Tesco £9.99

Converting to biodynamic
Into the garrigue again for another gorgeous, velvety, supple red.
Good to see wine of this quality on a supermarket shelf – if your
branch doesn't stock it they should be prepared to order it for you.

1995 LES BAUX-DE-PROVENCE, CUVÉE AURELIA
Domaine des Terres Blanches
Vintage Roots £10.75
Certified organic, vegan
Yet another firecracker from bauxite country, this wine has
aromas that reach out of the glass and grab your attention from
several paces. All that southern spice is yours, with plenty of
complexity in the seriously ripe fruit.

1995 PESSAC-LÉOGNAN
Château Haut-Nouchet
Vintage Roots £12.50
Certified organic, vegan
Classy organic red Bordeaux. Not much of that about. Vintage
Roots also stock Haut-Nouchet's white Pessac-Léognan, and this is
a worthy companion – rich, mouthfilling fruit, lively and elegant,
with complex, soft tannins lending structure. Really good example,
well worth putting on the table with anything that isn't fast food.

1998 MONTIRIUS GIGONDAS
Eric and Christine Saurel
Tesco £12.99
Converting to biodynamic
Described on the back label as being 'a big powerful wine packed
with layers of spicy ripe flavours – herbs, wild forest fruits and
raspberries predominate'. It is a big powerful wine, and full of
fruit. Whether you need to stray into the forest is up to you. I'd sit
back and enjoy a really good wine without worrying about the
wolf.

1997 CÔTES DE PROVENCE
Domaine de Marcoux
La Reserve £16.50
Certified organic, biodynamic

A huge wine, this, full of sweet ripe fruit; like one of those still-life fruit bowls come to life in your glass. It packs the punch of a boxing glove but is still well balanced and lively, with a loooong finish staying with you well after you've put down your glass (you have put down your glass, haven't you?).

1996 TERRA D'OR
Coteaux d'Aix-en-Provence
Chapoutier
Harrods, Michael Morgan, Gauntley's of Nottingham £29.99
Eco

I adored this, and to hell with the price. If I had to have a list of desert island wines the Terra d'Or would be in the final eight. It has such depth and concentration, the heady smells and intense flavours of Provence captured in the glass. It's a thick, dense gem, showing what great things happen when winemaker and land are one.

ITALY

1997 LA SEGRETA
Planeta
Valvona & Crolla £7.49
Eco

This just has to be one of the best-value Italian reds around. It's made from Nero d'Avola, one of the best Sicilian varieties, blended with Merlot. Rich, deep autumnal flavours (mushrooms and truffles, I mean, not mushy leaves) and a peppery nose. Brilliant with pasta or a big, rich cold-weather casserole (yes, all right, perfect for Wimbledon then). Planeta is a young, dynamic company and a name to watch.

1997 DOLCETTO D'ALBA
Viberti
Vintage Roots £7.95
Certified organic, vegan
Dolcetto is a very sensible counterpoint, for Italian winemakers, to the wines made from Barbera or Nebbiolo that demand long ageing. Dolcetto means 'little sweet one' but I fancy the sweetness refers more to the purse than the palate. It needs to be drunk young, within two or three years of the vintage as a rule, which has a happy effect on cashflow. Not only that, but it ripens up to a month earlier than Nebbiolo so it can be grown on less good vineyard sites, generating income from land that would otherwise be hard to use. And the wine works very well in the glass too – lots of lively fruit, easy to drink in large mouthfuls, and with that attractive hint of bitterness on the finish so common in Italy.

1996 CHIANTI CLASSICO
Buodonno
Vintage Roots £8.99
Certified organic, vegan
Classico refers to the heartland of Chianti, itself in the heartland of British holiday territory. This has an enticing nose, masses of creamy vanilla oak and ripe red fruit. Very concentrated. This really seems to be one of those wines that proves the point often made about organic wines – that they give a truer expression of the grape and soil. This wine is crystal clear and speaks loudly.

1996 REGIANO BARRIQUE
Perlage
Vinceremos, HDRA £8.99
Certified organic, vegan
Weighing in at a mighty 14 per cent alcohol, this is not a wine to

be quaffed lightly. The ageing for seven months in Slavonic oak doesn't exactly lighten things up, either. Maybe that's what gives it a slight, curious hint of eau-de-swimming-baths on the nose. Your tongue, on the other hand, will delight in the sweet ripe blackcurrant fruit, the long finish and the overall impression of surprising elegance. You'd probably be wise to open this well in advance, or decant it and really give it some air.

1997 DOLCETTO D'ALBA
Mauro Veglio
The Winery £9.50
Eco

Remarkably deeply coloured for Dolcetto. The depth of colour follows through into the palate, which is lush and rich. It's deep and well structured, and the tannins are already softening. Mauro Veglio is nothing if not an individualist, explaining to his importer why he hasn't bothered to go for organic certification. 'I make wine to make good wine. Why should I use the word organic as a marketing tool?' I think the only way to convince these guys that it's more than a marketing tool is for us customers to put pressure on suppliers for full information on the label. Meanwhile, certified or not, this wine has a lot to offer.

1995 FIOR DI SELVA BARRIQUE
Vinceremos, HDRA £9.99
Certified organic, vegan

Deep, intense fruit, a gutsy rich blend of Cabernet, Sangiovese and Canaiolo, with excellent concentration. Pungent farmyard smells on the nose (rotting cabbage leaves, manure) and lean, suave ripe fruit in the mouth with just a hint of hard tannin on the finish – a year or so in barriques sees to that. It has power, character and a long finish, and if you drink it now you'll wish you'd kept a few bottles to drink in three years' time. (Though I'll drink it now, happily, and often.) One of the keys to organic production, to my mind, should be the strengthening of regional character. Wine made to a price point tends to taste of nothing very much. Wines emphasising where they come from, offering individuality and character, are a world away from 'industrial' wines – and this Tuscan blockbuster offers a perfect example of that.

SPAIN

1998 TEMPRANILLO D'ANYADA, PENEDÈS
Albet i Noya
Vintage Roots £5.90
Certified organic, vegetarian
There's a weird, slight rubber glove quality on the nose, but please don't let that put you off. There's enough soft ripe plum fruit here to keep the biggest enthusiast happy; supple and wriggly, packing a punch.

1998 RIOJA LIVOR
Viña Ijalba
Vintage Roots £5.99
Certified organic
Very lean, very fruit-driven, this blend of Tempranillo and Gratiano offers good acidity and a nice balance. Nothing heavy here, just honest, refreshing flavours.

1997 RIOJA NOEMUS
Vinceremos, HDRA £5.99
Certified organic
Delicious: masses of sweet ripe fruit – lots of character here but not a typical 'elbows' Rioja, all power-punchy fruit and assertive oak. This is much more relaxed, and all the better for it.

1998 TEMPRANILLO
Albet i Noya
Vinceremos, HDRA £6.49
Certified organic, vegan
Deep purple in colour, betraying its youth, but it's highly tasty:
well-structured, rich fruit – blackberries, sour cherries. Soft and
already very approachable. If both vintages are still available, you
might like to compare this one with its older sibling listed below.

1997 TEMPRANILLO
Albet i Noya
Vinceremos, HDRA £6.49
Certified organic, vegan
A year older, the purple of the '98 is fading to ruby in the '97.
Taste is still good, though – cherry fruit here again, but I'd say
more morello than sour.

1997 PRIORATO
Mas Igneus
Vintage Roots £9.40
Certified organic, vegan
If you're looking for something that isn't run-of-the-mill, try this –
a blend of Grenache, Carignan and Cabernet Sauvignon. Hailing
from just west of Barcelona, and with a huge 14 per cent alcohol,
this is not a wine to be taken lightly. Very fragrant, the fruit is rich
and ripe and forward (why is it OK to call a wine forward without
it being thought a hussy?) and a lovely long finish. Yes OK, I
admit, I liked this.

1997 CABERNET SAUVIGNON COLLECCIO, PENEDÈS
Albet i Noya
Vintage Roots £10.25
The Albet i Noya brothers have a remarkable talent for extracting
intense, pure flavour from their grapes. This is textbook Cabernet,
so rich and satisfying with just the right amount of oak.
Winemaking at its best.

1996 SYRAH COL.LECCIO, PENEDÈS
Albet i Noya
Vintage Roots £10.99
Certified organic, vegan
A most unusual beast, a Spanish Syrah that more than gives the northern Rhône a run for its money. Very deep and dark with an extraordinary concentration of rich fruit, all plums and cherries and forest fruits. Wonderful now but with many years' life ahead.

GREECE

1997 PORFYROS
Domaine Spiropoulos
Oddbins £6.49; Vintage Roots £6.99
Certified organic, vegetarian
The major grape in this blend is the indigenous variety Agiorgitiko, blended with smaller amounts of Cabernet and Merlot, and it adds lively character to this rich, deep, languorous red. The Spiropoulos family finished organic conversion in 1996, one of the few Greek wineries to do so – though happily several others are in the process of converting and Oddbins, who stock several of them, will be happy to point you in their direction.

UNITED STATES

1997 ZINFANDEL
Fetzer Bonterra
Sainsbury's £8.49; Vinceremos, HDRA £8.99
Certified organic, vegan
The '96 may still be doing the rounds, but the '97 is worth looking out for: very intense chocolate/tobacco flavours. The winemakers proudly call this 'the Harley Davidson of wines – truly American', and indeed, what might a motorbike taste like?

1996 CABERNET SAUVIGNON
Fetzer Bonterra
Waitrose, Tesco, Oddbins, Sainsbury's, Fuller's, £8.99;
Vinceremos, HDRA £9.49; Vintage Roots £9.50
Certified organic, vegetarian
A very sweet rich nose, and spicy, soft ripe fruit on the palate,
possibly due to the small amount of Syrah they sneak in. Not a
typical big-time California red (and all the better for it).

1996 ZINFANDEL, NAPA VALLEY
Frog's Leap
Lay & Wheeler (01206 764446) £14.94
Certified organic, converting to biodynamic
John Williams of Frog's Leap welcomes visitors to his estate with a
'dirt tasting'. The contrast between his vineyard and his
neighbours' couldn't be more marked (see p. 35) and to
demonstrate the point he'll pick up a handful of earth from either
side of the track that separates them and invite you to smell the
difference (not taste, happily). He reckons his biodynamic methods
make for rich, sweet, vibrantly alive soil and the evidence is there
in the glass too. Not least in his Zinfandel, the grape claimed by
California as its own. The nose of this wine is fantastically potent
– it reaches out of the glass, grabs you by the throat and insists
you pay attention. It's magnificent. Sweet, spicy, minty, rich cigar
tobacco. The fruit is exquisite, lean and smoky, with perfectly
balanced tannins, wonderful juiciness. Terrific. Look out also for
good Cabernet and Merlot from this estate – excellent quality and
well worth drinking – but the Zinfandel is the star.

1993 CABERNET SAUVIGNON
Durney Vineyards
*Wine Merchants of Worcester £16.65; Upton-on-Severn Wines
(01684 592668) £17.01; Noble Rot Wine Warehouse £17.99;
Dickinsons of Hereford (01432 353720) £18.99*
Certified organic

Price is a factor in this California wine too. It seems much too
high. A lot of California wine is very steeply priced in the UK and
this is no exception – and, with this wine, I really don't feel it
warrants it. 'Dances on your palate', it says on the label. Dances
on your credit card, more like. It's ripe and rich and round, and
would be a good tenner's-worth – but nearly £19? I think not.

ARGENTINA

1996 COLOMÉ
Viñas de Davalos
Adnams £14.95
Eco

An extraordinary wine, coming to you from the foothills of the
Andes, claiming to be the highest vineyard in the world (2364
metres [7756 ft] if you must know). A heady collection of aromas
assaults the nose: liquorice, prunes, even a sort of tarriness. It's
dark, chewy and rich, throwing considerable sediment which
means no one's mucked about trying to fine or filter it, a great
sign. It comes from very old Cabernet and Malbec vines which are
ungrafted (in these days, when the phylloxera louse seems to have
dug its teeth into just about every ungrafted vine worldwide, this is
little short of a miracle). It'll keep and keep, but I for one wouldn't
be able to keep away from it. Argentina is making some very
interesting wines and I'm so pleased to find this uncertified organic
example. May there be more soon.

AUSTRALIA

1996 SHIRAZ MALBEC
Temple Bruer
Tesco £6.99
Converting to organic
This Aussie brandishes its heart on its sleeve. There's no subtlety here, it's a hit-you-between-the-eyes blend of 74 per cent Shiraz (Syrah) and 26 per cent Malbec. Very, very rich indeed.

1998 ORGANIC ORIGINS SHIRAZ/CABERNET SAUVIGNON
Robinvale Vineyard
Vintage Roots £7.75
Certified organic, vegan
Although an estate producing grapes biodynamically, Robinvale bought these grapes in from organic growers. So organic, but not biodynamic this time. This is the standard Aussie Cab/Shiraz blend but there's nothing standard about this wine. It's restrained, for one thing, in a most un-Oz way – no shouting strains of blackcurrant to make you think it's a kind of alcoholic Ribena. No, here we have a wine that's elegant and honest, without oak treatment so the fruit is allowed to speak for itself.

1997 PENFOLDS CLARE VALLEY CABERNET SHIRAZ
Selfridges, Safeway, Victoria Wine, Classic Wines £7.99
Certified organic, vegan
There's a minty, chocolate nose here, very After Eight, and that mintiness holds right through the wine to the finish. It was matured in new and newish French oak for seven months, and you're well aware of the oak adding depth and complexity to the rich ripe red-berry fruit. It's juicy and lively; drinking well now, but will keep if you can bear it. It's suitable for vegans because no fining agents were used. (Definitely approve of that.)

By the time you read this the '97 will be giving way to the '98, which is a Merlot/Cabernet/Shiraz blend. Be interesting to make the comparison if you get the chance.

1996 CABERNET MERLOT
Temple Bruer
Spar £7.99
Converting to organic
Stalky nose, lovely ripe dark-berry fruit and a hint of tobacco.
Good acidity to balance. A well-made, well-structured wine.
Excellent to see an organic wine peering round the door of Spar
shops too.

1996 RESERVE MERLOT
Temple Bruer
Tesco £9.99
Converting to organic
Gorgeous plummy Merlot in perfect balance, cherry pie with
pronounced new oak. Very stylish and altogether a damn fine
wine.

1993 CABERNET SAUVIGNON, MUDGEE
Thistle Hill Vineyard
Vintage Roots £10.99
Certified organic, vegan
Deeply coloured and thick, with an attractive meaty nose, it has
brilliant depth of fruit and a long, long finish. Like many an Aussie
Cabernet this is a powerful wine, but the punch it packs is
restrained by age and it's all the better for it ('93! Hard to find any
kind of ageing with organic wines at the moment, so this is
particularly interesting.)

1991 VIRGIN HILLS, VICTORIA
Domaine Gilbert
Vin du Van (01233 758727) £19.95
Eco
An intoxicating blend of Cabernet Sauvignon, Shiraz, Malbec and
Merlot (but an uncharacteristically modest, for Australia, indeed
practically un-intoxicating 11 per cent alcohol) this wine is truly

delicious: multi-layered, rich, round, with finesse and elegance which gives the lie to rough-and-ready Oz. And so it should, at a whisper under £20. Another rare chance to buy some well-aged organic wine. The '94s and '95s, when they come on stream, will be a fractionally lower £18.95. If you're looking for really low sulphur levels, seek this wine out: their aim is to keep sulphur below ten parts per million. That really *is* low.

NEW ZEALAND

1994 TE ARAI RIVER CABERNET MERLOT
Millton Vineyard
Vinceremos, HDRA £6.25
Eco, biodynamic, vegan

This is an interesting blend. Forty per cent of each of Merlot and Cabernet Sauvignon, plus 20 per cent Malbec and Cabernet Franc, each of which was fermented and aged separately – nearly two years of it, in French and American oak. Chocolate and peppermint aromas waylay you in the glass, and it follows through magnificently on the palate with excellent extract of lean, minty flavour and soft tannins. It's a very unusual, attractive wine, and will probably keep another five years if you can bear to let it.

SOUTH AFRICA

1998 CAPE SOLEIL CABERNET SAUVIGNON, PAARL DISTRICT
Sonop Wine Farm
Vintage Roots £5.85
Certified organic, vegan

I'm not a fan of the hugely blackcurranty style of Cabernet Sauvignon – you know, the kind that makes you think you may as well go and drink Ribena. Happily, this isn't one of those. The Cabernet here is restrained and the wine well structured, with soft tannins and very ripe fruit. The only certified organic wine estate in South Africa is performing well.

1996 JORDAN VINEYARDS MERLOT
Christopher Piper Wines £8.99
Eco

The Jordans learned their trade in California then brought their know-how back home to Stellenbosch. Organic winemakers are thin on the ground in South Africa, despite the countrywide initiative to reduce spraying, so this couple's juicy, characterful wines are very welcome. Vivid hints of chocolate on the nose, and chewy, oaky and tannic in the mouth, this is a wine well worth exploring.

SWEET WHITES

FRANCE

1996 SAUTERNES
Château la Garenne
Vinceremos, HDRA £9.99 (50 cl bottle)
Certified organic, vegan

With this organic Sauternes, France's top dessert-wine region finally gets a mention. This is really encouraging, especially as elsewhere in Bordeaux there seems to be so little interest in organics (or in good-value winemaking, either, but that's another story). And this is a very good example too. That characteristic noble-rot nose, smelling of honey and beeswax. The sweetness, when you taste it, isn't cloying or overwhelming. There's decent acidity here, and good structure (and hints of vanilla) from six months' ageing in new oak barrels. You'll certainly be able to keep this wine – whether or not you can resist it will be another matter.

1997 SAUSSIGNAC COUP DE COEUR
Château Richard
Vintage Roots £12.95 (50 cl bottle)
Certified organic, vegan
Everything you'd expect from Richard Doughty. Rich, honeyed
sweetness beautifully balanced by clean acidity. My notes mention
great legs, fab body and a huge finish. Yes of course it was the
wine I was talking about. Legs (or tears; let's calm down) are what
you call the lines left dripping down the glass after you've swirled
the wine around. Sweet wines don't get much better than this.

ROSE

FRANCE

1998/9 ORGANIC ROSÉ
Vin de Pays des Côtes de Thongue
Louis Delhon
Vintage Roots £4.25
Certified organic, vegan
Pale salmon pink, this tastes delightfully creamy and ripe – like
old-fashioned raspberry ripple. Or the strawberries my mother
used to freeze and then reconstitute as purée. It's robust and lively
on the palate, with an acidity that's attractively refreshing without
making its presence too assertively felt.

1998 COTEAUX DE PIERREVERT
Domaine Lablaque
La Reserve £5.50
Biodynamic
Tucked inland from the Côte d'Azure not far from Nice, this estate
is owned by an industrialist who bought it as a weekend retreat

and put a young winemaker in to tend the vines – money no object. Given a free hand and no money worries, the winemaker, Gilles Delsuc, has experimented and come up with a winning hand. A deep salmon pink, this blend of Syrah, Cinsault and Grenache is full and fat and round, with a long, long finish – really packing a punch.

1997 COTEAUX D'AIX-EN-PROVENCE
Mas de Gourgonnier
Organic Wine Company £5.99
Certified organic, vegetarian
Good deep colour and a creamy strawberry nose. Another good example, this, with its bouncy fresh fruit and long finish. Although you could (and indeed I could) quite comfortably sip this under a sunshade, it'll partner a fair range of food. Grilled salmon, say, or a lot of what passes for barbecue fodder.

1997 LA VIEILLE FERME ROSÉ
Côtes du Ventoux
Roberson £6.75
Converting to organic
Gorgeous deep salmon pink, you have bags of creamy strawberry fruit waiting for you here. In deepest southern France these vineyards face north, avoiding the ravages of summer heat; the south-facing slopes opposite the vines feature ochre-red earth, which the romantic in me feels is somehow appropriate for making a rosé. A blend of southern French varieties Cinsault, Grenache and Syrah, the wine is made by leaving the gently crushed grapes to macerate overnight. The red skins will impart just enough colour to give this salmon-pink hue without overpowering the delicate wine we want on a summer's afternoon. The following morning the juice is run off the skins and fermented.

So often with rosé – especially the cheap Cabernet-based supermarket versions – the acidity is enough to strip your teeth. It's very different here. The acidity is refreshing – which, after all, we need in the summer sun – but balanced with all this lovely ripe aromatic fruit. A real winner, and one I enjoy.

1998 COTEAUX LES BAUX-DE-PROVENCE
Domaine Terres Blanches
Vintage Roots £6.99
Certified organic, vegetarian
Exquisite cool creaminess, smooth and uncharacteristically elegant for a rosé. This contains finely balanced, sophisticated fruit, lots of juiciness and general benevolence.

CHAMPAGNE AND OTHER FIZZ

FRANCE

CLAIRETTE DE DIE TRADITION, MÉTHODE DIOISE ANCESTRALE
Achard-Vincent
Yapp (01747 860423) £7.25; Vinceremos £7.99
Certified organic, vegan
Die rhymes here with 'see'; it's a tiny town near the Rhône valley, towered over on both sides by imposing mountain ranges extending up past the snowline. The valley between, in which Die lies, marks the dividing line between alpine and Mediterranean climates. Made from Muscat à Petits Grains, it has that enticing Muscat nose, and lovely ripe, sweet fruit with more appley bite to balance. Only 7 per cent alcohol makes it a perfect aperitif.

CUVÉE LUDWIG HAHN
Guy Bossard
Organic Wine Company £7.95
Certified organic
Made mostly from the Muscadet grape, this is a wine of
extraordinary quality for the price – great depth and complexity,
nervy yet well balanced. I would never have expected this kind of
quality from a region dedicated to still-wine production. Try this –
I think you'll be impressed. I'd certainly crack a bottle given the
slightest provocation.

CLAIRETTE DE DIE BRUT
Achard-Vincent
Vinceremos, HDRA £7.99
Certified organic, vegan
This wine, on the other hand, is made from a blend of Clairette
and Muscat grapes and fermented to more normal alcoholic
strength. You'll find an aromatic, spicy nose, followed by fresh,
crisp, appley fruit. Off-dry and ripe and rather attractive.

SAUMUR BRUT
Gerard Leroux
Organic Wine Company £8.49
Certified organic, vegetarian
Saumur, one of the most attractive towns on the Loire, specialises
in sparkling wine made from Chenin Blanc. You couldn't guess the
grape variety from this wine, which is pretty neutral in taste, and
not that good in terms of value for money, but it's light-bodied
and refreshing – a good swig, or a base wine for kir royale.

CHAMPAGNE JEAN BLIARD
Organic Wine Company £15.89
Certified organic
It's interesting. The Organic Wine Company stock two
Champagnes from Bliard. One is a Cuvée des Trois Cépages,

which means it's blended from all three of the permitted
Champagne grape varieties – Chardonnay, Pinot Noir and Pinot
Meunier. The other is a Blanc de Blancs, white made from whites,
i.e. a fizz made only from white grapes – Chardonnay, in other
words.

Unfortunately the wine label doesn't reveal which of the two this
is. (Though it does reveal very questionable taste in labels. Well, a
creeper-covered wall and lacy net curtains? I might love my home
but I wouldn't necessarily put a photo of it on my wine label.)

Happily their taste in Champagne is irreproachable, so the
answer is to encase the bottle in a Rapid-Ice, so you don't have to
see the wretched label, and simply pour and enjoy. I worked out
from the taste of this wine that it must be the Trois Cépages blend,
made from both red and white grapes, because it's a really rich,
deep wine – full, concentrated, long long finish. Blanc de Blancs
tend to be racier, lighter, leaner. This really is highly
recommendable – it knocks spots off many of the Champagne
brand names we all know *and* for a much more reasonable price
and it's organic.

CHAMPAGNE VEUVE FOURNY ET FILS
Berry Brothers & Rudd Ltd £16.45
Eco
Another Blanc de Blancs, made entirely from Chardonnay, this
wine has the raciness and zing of acidity you might expect. It also
has a very desirable fullness and depth.

CHAMPAGNE FLEUR DE L'EUROPE
Eugène Fleury
Vintage Roots £18.99
Certified biodynamic, vegan
Fleury grows his grapes biodynamically, which is as rare as hens'
teeth in Champagne. And I wish, I really do, that I could rave
about the results, but I can't. I'm sorry to say it didn't do much for
me. And at that price it needs to. Go for this if it has to be

biodynamic, by all means, but for well-made, good-value organic fizz you'll need to look elsewhere.

SPAIN

1995 CAVA BRUT RESERVA
Albet i Noya
Vintage Roots £8.65
Certified organic, vegan
Cava is Spain's answer to Champagne – made the same way, with second fermentation in bottle. This one is lively and refreshing, a light style that's off-dry and yeasty, with plenty of flavour and a touch of roundness from that extra bottle age. (Interesting how roundness does come with age, isn't it?) And at half the price of Grand Marque Champagne, a good-value alternative.

A FINAL WORD

'... modern technology will have made its mark well before the vine is planted: lasers can be used to level the land with perfect precision, and vine rows established with equal care; computer-controlled irrigation will have been installed in advance, and the vines given an exactly measured quantity of water within hours of planting; the soil may have been fumigated against nematodes, and herbicides will ensure they begin life without any competition from grass or weeds.'

James Halliday and Hugh Johnson,
The Art and Science of Wine

We have a choice.

We can support chemical-based agriculture and viticulture by buying its products. We can buckle under and meekly buy GM food and drink. Or we can choose to put our money on the table in support of organic producers. Money talks. We as consumers have enormous, undreamed-of power. The supermarkets' hasty backtracking on GM foods in the spring of 1999 is just one proof of that. The huge increase in turnover in organic food and drink is another, being catered for by the promise of dozens more organic supermarkets.

The tide is changing, and we're all part of that. I look forward to the day when it's no longer organic wine that is singled out with special labels, but the stuff made by spraying it to death first. 'Contains pesticides' will appear as a kind of government health warning, of the sort that cigarettes carry now.

It's up to us.

GLOSSARY

AC, Appellation d'origine contrôllée
Supposedly the top rung of the quality ladder in France. Should be a guarantee of quality but of course it isn't. The same applies to DOC in Italy, DO in Spain, QmP in Germany etc.

Anthroposophy
The 'spiritual science' developed by Rudolf Steiner, the Austrian mystic who created biodynamics.

Bacillus thuringiensis
Abbreviated as Bt, this bacteria forms the basis of an organic pesticide. Its effectiveness is now threatened by genetic engineering.

Bactericides
Chemicals to kill bacteria.

Biodiversity
Maintaining a wide range of species of all living things. Under threat from many sources.

Biodynamic
A form of organic viticulture that seeks to heal the earth by using homeopathy, planetary influences and the grape grower's thoughts and awareness. See Chapter 6.

Blanc de blancs
Literally 'white of whites', signifying a white wine made from white grapes. 'Blanc de noirs' is a white wine made from black grapes.

Bordeaux mixture
Mix of copper sulphate, lime and water, much used to control fungal disease. Although permitted for organic use, it needs to be used with care to prevent toxic copper build-up in the soil.

Botrytis cinerea
Grey rot, to any gardener, is very undesirable; but to grape growers wishing to make sweet white wine it's a godsend. The tiny fungal filaments of the rot pierce the grape skin, and the sun then evaporates the grape's water content through the holes, leaving only unctuous sweet juice.

Bt
See *Bacillus thuringiensis*.

Cave
French cellars.

Chaptalisation
Adding sugar to fermenting wine to make up for deficiencies in under-ripe, low-sugar grapes – 'the sun in a bag'. Many growers pretend they don't do it, but do; many organic regulations forbid it.

Château
Posh name for wine estate.

Cloning
Growing identical siblings from a few vines chosen for high yield or good flavour.

Composting
Turning garden and kitchen waste into soil nutrients to add to the vines.

Conventional winemaking/grape growing
Used in this book to describe all these new-fangled ideas involving the use of lots of chemicals and mucking about with natural processes.

Conversion
Moving from conventional to organic winemaking. Usually takes three years for the soil to recover from the use of chemical sprays. After the first year of conversion the wine's 'in conversion' status can be mentioned on the label.

Cru
Literally 'growth'. Used in France to denote superior quality wine. Beaujolais has top 'cru' villages, Bordeaux and Burgundy have complicated systems of crus denoting a quality ladder.

DDT
An insecticide once popular and widely used, and now banned because its deadly effects on humans are now recognised. And where it led, many other insecticides and pesticides have followed. Including many still used illegally on our food today.

Downy mildew
Fungal disease, also known as peronospera. Prevent by spraying with copper.

Eco
Term used in this book to denote wine made to organic standards but not officially certified.

Ecology
The study of consequences. Understanding the effects of use of chemicals, for example. Seeking balance.

Erosion, soil
The washing-away of topsoil by poor viticulture and agriculture practices.

Faire pisser les vignes
Literally 'to make the vines piss': over-watering, or allowing too many bunches of grapes to form on the vine. Both lead to dilution of grape juice and therefore of flavour.

Fanleaf virus
One of the oldest-known virus diseases of the vine, often spread by nematode worms – scourge of California.

Fertiliser
Adds nutrients to the soil.

Filtering
Removing particles from the wine before bottling – a physical process of passing the wine through a filter or sieve.

Fining
Removing particles from the wine by adding matter – clay, egg whites, fish bladders – and letting that matter precipitate out of the wine with the particles attached.

Frankenstein food
Food containing genetically modified organisms.

Friends of the Earth
Campaigning group for the environment.
Fungicide
Chemical to kill fungus.
Genes
Building blocks of all life forms.
Gene tinkering
Playing God with building blocks of all life forms.
Genetic manipulation
Ditto.
Genetic modification
Ditto.
Genetically engineered
Ditto.
Glyphosate
Active ingredient of the world's favourite herbicide, Roundup.
GM/GMO
Genetically modified organism.
Grafting
Cutting new shoots on to vine rootstocks. Nearly all the world's vines are grafted on to American rootstocks that show resistance to the louse phylloxera, which devastated vineyards in the late nineteenth century.
Greenpeace
Ecologically oriented campaign group, currently fighting the introduction of GMOs.
Henry Doubleday Research Association
Organic gardening association (see page 115).
Herbicide
Chemical that kills weeds (and also crops, unless they're genetically engineered to resist it).
Homeopathy
Treats disease with substances in massive dilutions.
IFOAM
International Federation of Organic Agriculture Movements.

Umbrella body acting as international resource agency.

Insecticides

Chemicals to kill insects.

Kabinett

The first rung on the German wine quality ladder. Kabinett wines are generally relatively light and fresh compared to heavier-weight wines such as late harvested and special selection (Spätlese and Auslese).

Lazarus gene

Aka Terminator 2. Chemical to bring specially engineered seeds back to life the following season (on payment of a fee to the chemical company, of course). See pages 67–68.

Lees

Spent yeast cells that fall to the bottom of the vat after giving their all during fermentation. Some wines, notably Muscadet, benefit from a winter 'sur lie' – on the lees – which gives this neutral grape some zing and yeasty freshness.

Malolactic fermentation

A fermentation in wine that turns sharper appley malic acid into softer lactic acid. Some wines benefit from this, others don't.

Methyl bromide

Fumigant – clears the soil of nematodes.

Miticide

Chemical to kill mites.

Must

The mix of grape juice, skins, stems, pips and pulp which results immediately after the grapes have been crushed at the start of the winemaking process.

MW, Master of Wine

Highest rung of the wine trade's qualification ladder.

Nematicides

Chemicals to kill nematodes – see below.

Nematode worms

Microscopic worms, many of which feed on grapevine roots and cause a lot of damage, or transmit virus diseases.

Nitrogen
The essential element in most fertilisers. Growers restrict nitrogen levels to produce top-quality grapes.

Oidium
French name for powdery mildew.

Organic
Wines made without the use of artificial fertilisers or chemical sprays, and with lower sulphur levels than conventional wines.

Pasteurisation
Heating the wine to a temperature – 85°C – that kills all micro-organisms such as yeasts and bacteria. A pretty brutal technique, and one that should only be used on wines with no potential to age in the bottle.

Pesticides
Chemicals that kills insects. The name implies they only kills pests; try telling that to all the butterflies, bees and beneficial insects that fall foul of them.

Pharming
Playing God with genes, the building blocks of all life forms.

Pheromone traps
Sticky insect traps that attract males by wafting forth the smell of females. The males, lured by the smell, are trapped and thus unable to mate and propagate.

Phylloxera vastatrix
Root-feeding aphid that munched its way through the world's vine-yards in the nineteenth century. Phylloxera vastatrix ('the devastator') has no known cure (although biodynamics is claiming some success against it). The only protection is to graft the variety you want to grow on to resistant rootstocks.

Powdery mildew
Aka oidium. A fungal disease which likes to lurk and grow under dense leaf canopies. So either keep the canopy cut back or spray with sulphur.

Racking
Siphoning the wine off its lees or sediment.

Recombinant DNA
Playing God with genes, the building blocks of all life forms.

Rootstock
The roots and base stem on to which the desired vine variety is grafted. To deter phylloxera, rootstocks are normally American vines.

Roundup-Ready
Plants which have been genetically modified to resist the herbicide Roundup, made by Monsanto.

Sec
Dry.

Soil Association
Organisation supporting and regulating organic agriculture and viticulture in the UK.

Steiner, Rudolf
Austrian scientist and seer who developed biodynamics.

Sulphur
The one chemical it's almost impossible for a winemaker – organic or conventional – to do without. See pages 52–55.

Sustainable
Maintaining a balance between what's put in and what's taken out. Conventional agriculture and viticulture degrades the soil and pollutes our drinking water through intensive chemical use. Sustainable agriculture seeks to minimise its impact on the environment.

Systemic
Taken by the vine into its system. With chemicals, that means residues can persist after spraying.

Tartrates
Harmless crystals thrown by wine during fermentation and maturation. A sign of un-mucked-about-with wine.

Terminator gene
Genetic modification that ensures a plant's seed is sterile, forcing farmers to buy fresh seed each year instead of saving from the previous crop.

Terminator 2
See Lazarus gene.

Terroir
A French concept meaning a sense of place, of a wine's origin, of 'somewhereness'.

Vinification
Winemaking.

Viticulture
Grape growing.

Vitis vinifera
The species of vine from which most of the world's wine is made. Susceptible to phylloxera, so these days it is grafted on to non-vinifera rootstock.

TASTING TERMS

Acidity
The fresh or tart taste of the acids in wine. They need to be in balance with the sugars in the wine: if the acidity is too high in relation to the sugars, you'll taste too much acid; the wine will be tart, 'acidic', not pleasant to drink.

Astringent
Tannin can sometimes have this mouth-drying effect; present in particular in some Italian reds.

Balanced
Acidity, alcohol, flavours, sugars … all the elements in pleasing harmony with each other.

Body
Can be light, medium or full: this is about the 'weight' of the wine, how much of a punch of flavour and alcohol it packs.

CFDN
Crisp, fresh, dry, neutral: my personal abbreviation for wines I see too much of in big tastings, white wines made cheaply and in large volume that have no faults but no personality either. Happily organic wines tend to express themselves better than this, so it's an

abbreviation I haven't had to use much in this book. Which is nice.

Corked, corky
Nothing to do with bad bottle opening leaving bits of cork floating in the wine, this describes a musty, dusty taint in the wine from a faulty cork.

Correct
No faults, nothing wrong with it – just not very interesting. A bit of a put-down, for me.

Crisp
Pronounced, lively acidity.

Elbows
A blockbuster of a wine.

Fat
Mouthfilling, luscious.

Firm
Pretty high tannin or acidity, but usually a young wine that will mature into something kinder and more approachable.

Fresh
What a nice young white wine should be; lively, with good acidity.

Length
How long the impression of a wine remains in your mouth after you've spat or swallowed. The longer, the better, as a rule.

Mature
Drink it now; it won't improve further.

Oaky
The taste that comes from barrel fermenting or ageing (or, for cheapskates, from bunging a bag of oak chips into the wine). Can be very pronounced, especially in some New World wines, and over-oaked wines hide all the fruit and taste of nothing but barrel, which is deeply tedious.

Oily
A characteristic smell of good, mature Riesling.

Petillance
Slight spritz, a lightly sparkling wine.

Petrolly
Another characteristic Riesling whiff.
Rounded
Well balanced.
Short
Opposite of long. Obviously. Means there isn't too much going on here.
Structure
How all the various elements of the wine come together (or don't).
Tannic
Tannins come from grape skins, pips and stalks, and from the wood in which the wine is aged. Tannic wines taste bitter and astringent, even mouth-puckering. Tannins help the wine age, and 'hard' tannins you encounter in a young wine will, if the wine has been made correctly, eventually soften and add an extra dimension to the wine.
Weight
Describes the amount of flavour, the 'presence' of the wine in the mouth.

USEFUL ADDRESSES AND WEBSITES

Website addresses for supermarkets and specialist wine retailers are given with their main entries in Chapter 8.

WINERIES

Many wineries now have websites, and the number increases almost daily. A good place to check out the latest updates is at www.vine2wine.com which regularly cleans its lists of links and currently boasts 'over 2400 links to wine sites on the net'.

Bonterra: www.bonterra.com
Chapoutier: www.chapoutier.com
Comte Cathare: www.comtecathare.com
Durney: www.usawines.com/durney
Frog's Leap: www.frogsleap.com
Glenara: www.glenara.com.au
Jordan: www.wineroute.co.za/Jordan.html
Chateau Musar: www.chateaumusar.com.lb
Penfolds: www.Penfolds.com
Perrin: www.vinternet.net/Beaucastel
Pieropan: www.pieropan.it
Spiropoulos: www.addgr.com/wine/arkas/company.htm
Thevenet: www.terroirs-b.com/labongran

PRESSURE GROUPS AND ORGANIC ORGANISATIONS

www.ecowine.com

This site is run by another, more proactive company, the Organic Wine Company. They're based in San Francisco and sell to US customers, but anyone can subscribe to an interesting, motivational e-zine written by MD Veronique Raskin who founded the company in 1980.

www.reninet.com/catz

The website for CATS, Californians for Alternatives to Toxics. Plenty here to scare you about pesticide over-use.

http://ecoweb.dk/ifoam

Here you'll find the homepage of IFOAM, the International Federation of Organic Movements. Not always fascinating, but often some useful campaigning pages.

www.soilassociation.org

Bristol House, 40–56 Victoria Street, Bristol BS1 6BY
Phone: 0117 929 0661
Fax: 0117 925 2504
The Soil Association campaigns for organic farming. If you want to join a box scheme, they'll sell you a list. Not much doing on the wine front, though, and their public front sometimes seems to buckle under the strain of huge recent expansion to cope with the upswing in interest.

www.hdra.org.uk

Henry Doubleday Research Association (HDRA), Europe's largest organic organisation. See main entry on page 115.

www.foe.co.uk

Friends of the Earth
FREEPOST, 56–58 Alma Street, Luton, Beds LU1 2YZ
Friends of the Earth are another campaigning outfit on green

issues, and have been at the forefront of anti-GM campaigning. To get the latest updates on the US Supreme Court case attempting to halt the use of Bt in genetically modified crops, contact: Charles Margulis, Greenpeace Genetic Engineering Campaign, 1817 Gough Street, Baltimore, MD 21231, USA

charles.margulis@dialb.greenpeace.org

BIODYNAMIC AGRICULTURAL ASSOCIATION (BDAA)

Rudolf Steiner House, 35 Park Road, London NW1 6XT

Phone: 01453 759501

You can join the BDAA to learn more about biodynamics and to receive their newsletter *Star and Furrow*. They're actually based somewhere in the West Midlands, but the London address they use, Rudolf Steiner House, is a focal point for courses devoted to all aspects of Steiner's work. Rudolf Steiner House also contains an excellent bookshop, for those who want to rush out and buy *Agriculture* . . . They sell Maria Thun's planting calendar too, and also the much more user-friendly, larger format American version, *Stella Natura* (though if you buy this one, be prepared to sit down and work out the time zone difference!). Websites? Well, the UK organisations hasn't quite got that far, but there are some informative US sites:

www.biodynamics.com

www.demeter-usa.org

www.anthropsophy.com

SEDLESCOMBE VINEYARD

Cripp's Corner, Sedlescombe, Robertsbridge, East Sussex TN32 5SA

Phone: 01580 830715

Fax: 01580 830122

Website: www.tor.co.uk/sedlescombe/

INDEX

acidity in wines 61
Agriculture (Steiner, R.) 73, 74
ambiguousness in organic production 22–23
Argentina 102, 175
Australia 14, 102, 145–147, 176–178
Austria 94, 142

bacillus thuringiensis 68–69
benefits of wine consumption 12–14
biodynamics 73–87
Blue, Bob (Bonterra) 42–43, 53, 99
Bonterra at Fetzer (California) 98–100

carcinogens 9
certification of organic products 17–20
Chapoutier, Michel (Rhône wine-maker) 19, 73
chemicals, dependence on 33
chemicals, dangers of 9–11, 40–42
Chile 101–102
Cochran, Veronique (Château Falfas) 19, 81
compost 82–83
conversion to organic production 20–22
coronary heart disease 13
costs of production 42–43
Cyprus 97

DDT 10
definition of 'organic' 16–17Demeter 94
disease in vinyards 38–39
Doughty, Richard (Château Richard) 28, 31–32, 45, 55, 57–58, 59–60, 76

Eastern Europe 97
Eden, Robert (Comte Cathare) 20
England 105
environmental strategies 99–100

farming methods 28–49
fermentation, malolactic 55–56
fermentation, process of 51–52
filtering 58–60
fining 56–58
Food and Drink 11
France 89–91, 126–130, 132–140, 149–154, 156–168, 179–185

fungus 39–40

Gardener, Jem (Vinceremos) 88
Gardening by the Stars and Constellations (Thun, M.) 81
genetic manipulation 64–66
genetic modification 66–68, 69–72
Geoffroy, Jean-Baptiste (Champagne grower) 24
Germany 92–94, 141–142
Greece 96, 132, 143, 173
The Guardian 41–42

hangovers 14–15
harvesting 43–46
historical perspective 46–49
Hochar, Serge (Château Musar) 119–120
homeopathy 83–84
Hughes, Trevor (T&W Wines) 86–87, 119

independent wine merchants 117–121
integrated pest management (IPM) 24–25
integrated production of wine (IPW) 26–27
intensive farming 30–31
irrigation 33–36
Italy 91–92, 130–131, 140–141, 154–155, 168–171

Joly, Nicolas (Loire wine-maker) 65, 83
Jordan, Dr. Tony (Wirra Wirra Winery) 70–71

Kemp, Cheryl (Biodynamic Farming and Gardening Association of Australia) 102–103

labelling 111–112
Lebanon 105
Leflaive, Anne-Claude (Domaine Leflaive) 19
Liebig, Justus von 47
life-forces 76–77, 80–82
Loftus, Simon (Adnams) 18, 19, 59, 118
lunar influence 79–80
lutte raisonnée 24

Millton, James (New Zealand wine-maker) 22–23, 28–30, 45, 51, 82, 103–104
minerals for vines 37

New Zealand 22–23, 103–104, 147–149, 178
nutrients for vines 37–38

pasteurisation 55
pesticide, organic 68–69
pesticides *see* chemicals
pests 38–39
Pigott, Lance (Vintage Roots) 12
pollution, biodynamics as counter to 75
Portugal 96
price of organic wines 109–111
purity in vineyards 42

rhythms of nature 77–78
rules for organic cultivation 21–22

science and biodynamics 85–86
Scott, Dr. Nigel (molecular biologist) 70
soil and fertility 30–31, 82
solar influence 78–79
South Africa 26, 104, 149, 178–179
Spain 95, 131–132, 142–143, 155, 171–173, 185
specialist organic vintners 113–117
Steiner, Rudolf 74
sugar content 61
sulphur 14–15, 50, 52–55
Sunday Telegraph 11
supermarkets 108, 121–125
Switzerland 105

tartrates 60–61
taste 11–12
terminator gene 67–68
trace elements 58

United States 97–101, 143–144, 173–175

Vinceremos 114
vitis vinifera 63

water, biodynamic preparation and 84–85
weeds 36–37
Williams, John (Frog's Leap) 25, 35
Wine, The Art and Science of (Halliday, J. and Johnson, H.) 186
wine-making, good practice in 50–51

zodiacal influence 79